"The first time I saw Tiffanie Turner's breathtaking creations I did a double take. 'Paper? Impossible!' And yet sure enough, they are. And as such, they are utterly spectacular. *The Fine Art of Paper Flowers* is an in-depth instructional book for us mortals—super detailed with everything you need to know to try your hand at paper flower creation."

—ARIELLA CHEZAR, author of *The Flower Workshop*

"Tiffanie Turner's thoughtful approach to creating stunning, botanically accurate flowers is both inspiring and encouraging, opening our eyes to new ideas to create something of our own. From 'very easy' to 'not very hard,' her unique techniques take away the fear, making us want to pick up some crepe paper and make some flowers for our next party!"

—JAN HALVARSON and EARL EINARSON, founders of Poppytalk.com

THE FINE ART OF
paper flowers

A guide to making beautiful and lifelike botanicals

TIFFANIE TURNER

PHOTOGRAPHS BY
Tiffanie Turner
and
Aya Brackett

WATSON·GUPTILL
CALIFORNIA | NEW YORK

For my sweet
Stella and Oliver.

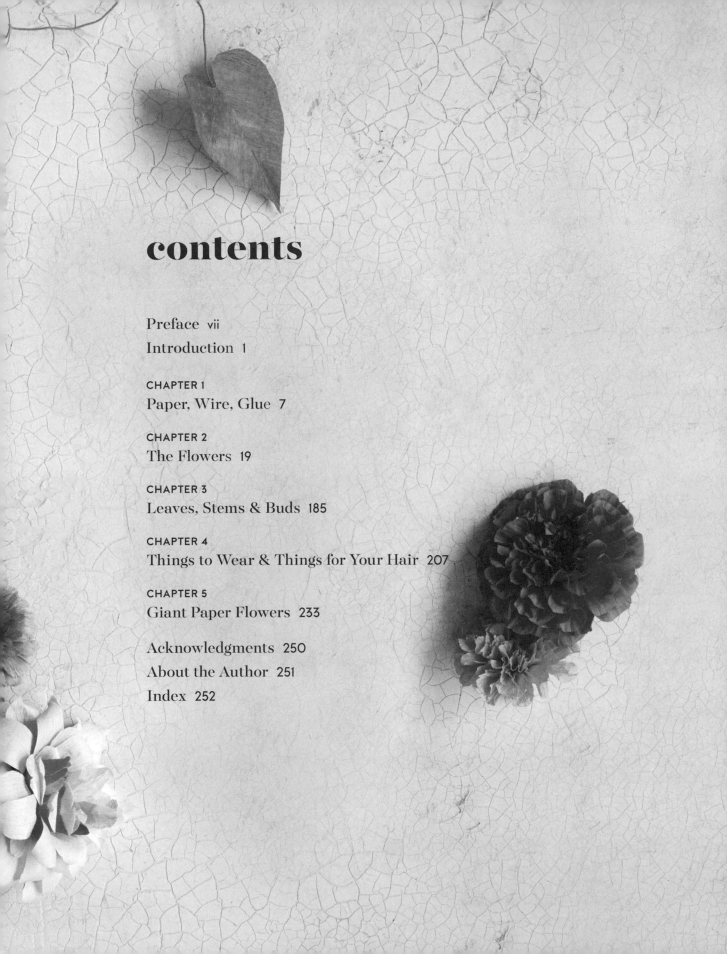

contents

preface

I have always been drawn to botanical artwork. From the full-color realism of a simple North American seed packet illustration to the artful accuracy of sliced-through stamens engraved by English and French botanists for early scientific plant studies to the moody, multiseasonal bouquets painted in the Netherlands in the seventeenth and eighteenth centuries, I find the depiction of plant life in art absolutely captivating. Now, after many years of daily practice, I have found the way I can best create my own botanical art: with paper.

While I have a deep and vested interest in botany, I cannot claim any sort of expertise in the subject. My knowledge of what exists in the world of flowers comes from years of nature wandering, garden coveting, book and image hoarding, and conversations with flower nerds like myself. My head is constantly spinning with flowers I've yet to make. When I create a certain flower in paper, I do a bit of research on how it grows, its place of origin, and the season in which it blooms. I will do my best as I go along to understand its form and structure, but you won't find me referencing the Fibonacci spiral or calling out specimens by their Latin names. I use the constructs of botany as a framework to express myself. So, while I am not a botanist, I do feel comfortable calling myself a botanical artist. I depict the appearance of different plants, mostly flowers, to some degree of accuracy, in paper.

If someone had told me five years ago that I was headed toward a career as a fine artist, instructor, and author on the subject of paper flowers, I wouldn't have believed them. Somehow, my time as an architect, an amateur botanical painter, an East Coast native, a twenty-year San Francisco resident, a flamenco student and burlesque performer, and a wife and mother, combined with being in the right place at the right time, all lead me here. I love costumes and fashion. I love art. I love performing. I love structure and building things. I love paper. I love glue. And I love flowers. It has all come together almost seamlessly, but I never could've planned it.

I wrote this book to share my own interpretation of the time-honored art and craft of paper flower making. I am self-taught, fueled by my curiosity about the natural world, an eye for detail, and my knowledge of construction and how things are built through my work as an architect. My work explores the incredible rhythms and patterns in nature. It takes things you might not notice, like the shape of the smallest floret of a flower, and brings them right to your face. I like my work to be realistic, without seeking to fool you completely. And while I possess such great respect for Mother Nature, sometimes it's important to mix things up, for flower petals to feel like feathers, reading first and foremost as whimsical bursts of color and texture. But the root for me is always botany.

This book fills a niche that had been empty when I sat down to write it, focusing exclusively on my medium of choice: crepe paper. Included are all of my techniques and philosophies, as well as all the things I've learned from working with my students. This is my attempt to do my little part in continuing to elevate this art. I am leaving all of my tips and tricks here, to open up space in my mind for new work, and to teach other paper flower lovers everything I've learned so far.

introduction

For the past four or five years, I have spent most of my days and nights standing in a pile of paper scraps in our San Francisco flat, making paper flowers big and small. Because we are in close quarters, everyone in my unbelievably patient family has had a role in my career as a paper artist, whether as an idea person, a janitor, or both. This book, which provides instruction on how to make all of my favorite crepe-paper flowers, as well as some wonderful projects using the flowers to adorn your body and home, is the fruit of that labor. As seriously as I take this craft, paper flower making is far from rocket science. While I give detailed instructions and specific techniques for making botanically accurate specimens in this book, I really want you to enjoy the journey and feel free to be creative. The supplies needed are simple and few in number. When I first started making flowers, I worked with the same range of supplies I do now: a roll of crepe paper, a length of wire, and a bit of glue. If you can't wait for crepe to arrive in the mail, start with bougainvillea made of party streamers. If you are out of wire, grab a coat hanger or wooden skewer. There are more materials available on the market than I use myself, and doing the work of creating paper flowers, using your hands, and learning the process are more important than using the perfect supplies.

I encourage you to approach each flower as a project unto itself. The tutorials range from "very easy" to "not very hard with a little practice." There are flowers in this book that can take five minutes, and a few that can take five hours or more. They have been grouped primarily by the techniques you will use to make them, which loosely relate to how they grow botanically. If this is your first foray into paper flower making, start with the tutorials in "Basic Techniques & Starter Specimens" (page 21) and then the hybrid tea rose tutorial (page 59) from "My Favorite Roses." These should build your confidence fairly quickly, but be patient with yourself at first, and use artistic license when you need to.

The biggest piece of advice I give to my students and anyone else seeking my help with paper flower making has always been this:

In order to achieve the desired results when working in realism, you must make what you see, not what you think you see.

This means working from real floral specimens, or even flowers depicted in art, whenever possible and trying to not get lost in the repetition in the form of a flower when so many flowers are actually quite irregular. It means paying attention to the details and the organized chaos that is nature and avoiding making assumptions when trying to re-create the natural world. There are as many glitches in the head of a flower as there are orderly rows of petals, which I try to recognize in my work. To assist in this, I spend a good deal of time in the tutorials talking about how to groom the petals in just the right ways, stretching, folding, and often crumpling the paper so that it catches the light and the petals appear as they would in nature. Several of the tutorials walk you through petal placement to help you attach them in the most realistic patterns and avoid the look of a flower made on an assembly line. Details like these mean a lot to me, and if you pay attention to them I promise you great results. My hope is that you will learn the skills to capture flowers the way you see them and that you will parlay those skills into making your own templates and techniques for new flowers and creations, if you so desire.

A LITTLE ABOUT THE FLOWERS

The flowers I have included in this book all have a certain je ne sais quoi. While I feel that some things are better off left to nature, these are the flowers that have spoken to me, the ones I knew I could do a certain amount of justice to. I have history with each of them. The Green Trick dianthus, for example, is a flower I might've never even considered until a bride asked me for Seussian tufts for her wedding bouquet and boutonnieres. I hadn't thought of making a dandelion or echinacea flower until I was in my home state of New Hampshire for a weeklong artist's residency and had time outside of my everyday life to explore and try new things. Most of these flowers I have made with the intention to wear, to be woven into a crown or just tucked behind my ear. All of the flowers in this book make my heart skip a beat or two, and I hope they strike a special chord with you, too.

HOW TO USE THIS BOOK

Reading through the information in chapter 1 "Paper, Wire, Glue" can help you become more familiar with the materials and why I use them, and identify the few simple items you should always have on hand. Chapter 2, "The Flowers" contains descriptions of the basic techniques used throughout the book, and all of the flower tutorials. The tutorials are separated into five sections, with the corresponding templates and

guides at the end of each section. Use the index to find the specific flower you may be looking for, as they are not all in alphabetical order. Although I enjoy working with the wide variety of crepe-paper colors in their natural state, chapter 2 also contains four special technique sections demonstrating how to work with color and treat the paper in different ways. While not always necessary for a completed flower, leaves and other green bits and buds can be found in chapter 3, "Leaves, Stems & Buds." The projects included in chapter 4, "Things to Wear & Things for Your Hair" are based on costume work I have done for my own performances, items I have made for some beautiful brides, and headpieces I have on hand to throw on whenever I see fit. Most of the flowers have been designed to be durable for long-lasting wear.

The flowers in this book are meant to be close to the size that they appear in nature. If you desire to make something larger, play with enlarging the templates, as well as the number of petals to be sure to fill out the flower's larger form. If you want something enormous, head straight to the end of the book, where you will find chapter 5, "Giant Paper Flowers." These are delicate but bold, feminine, and gigantic, and the bread and butter of my fine-art career.

I find inspiration for making paper flowers everywhere I look—vintage wallpapers and hotel carpets, old and new books, museums, fashion magazines, and, of course, in the garden. There is no shortage of source material and specimens for the paper flower enthusiast to work from. My greatest wish is that this book becomes a source of inspiration for you.

"Let every artist strive to make his flower a
beautiful living thing, something that will
convince the world that there may be, there
are, things more precious more beautiful—
more lasting than life itself. . . . You must
offer the flowers of the art that is in you—the
symbols of all that is noble—and beautiful—
and inspiring—flowers that will often change
a colourless leaf—into an estimated and
thoughtful thing."

—CHARLES RENNIE MACKINTOSH

CHAPTER 1

paper, wire, glue

all about crepe paper

Crepe paper is like candy to me; I cannot resist it. I love the feel of it in my hands, and my love of the colors drives my work almost as much as my love of flowers. I also love using it because it is incredibly durable, which ensures that the flowers I make will last. Each tutorial in this book calls out the weight and color of crepe you should use, along with alternate suggestions, but keeping rolls of white, yellow, and green crepe on hand will ensure you can make some version of almost any flower in the book.

Paper color-naming conventions are not consistent from supplier to supplier. Italian 60 and 180 gram crepe papers are identified by a number assigned by the manufacturer. I use that manufacturer's number along with a general color name I have assigned each when specifying Italian papers. Chinese 100 and 180 gram papers are called out by the manufacturer's color names and have no color numbers, so when you see "100 gram" or "180 gram" followed by a color name with no color number, that is Chinese paper. German 90 gram doublette and 160 gram crepe also have no color numbers and are called out by the supplier's color names.

CREPE PAPER TYPES

The following are the types of crepe paper I use in my work and are used throughout this book. Sources for each type of crepe paper are listed on pages 16 and 17.

180 gram Italian florist crepe
Specified by weight, manufacturer's color number, and a general color name (for example, 180 gram #600 white).

This is the heaviest and thickest crepe I use. The colors are vibrant, with a huge selection to choose from. It is the only crepe paper currently available in ombré colors, which I adore. It is almost impossible to rip without a struggle. Because it is so rigid and durable, I use it for the giant paper flowers at the end of this book. Many of the life-size flowers are made from it as well, either left textured and thick or stretched to be smooth and thin.

180 gram "Extra Heavy" Chinese crepe
Specified by weight and the manufacturer's color name (for example, 180 gram white).

Seemingly lighter in weight and more muted in color than its Italian counterpart, I use 180 gram "Extra Heavy" Chinese crepe primarily for a few unique colors it comes in that are hard to find in other weights.

160 gram German florist crepe
Specified by weight and the supplier's color name (for example, 160 gram white).

Lighter weight than the 180 gram Chinese crepe, but slightly stiffer. The colors are bright but natural. This crepe has the widest selection of greens.

100 gram "Heavy" Chinese crepe
Specified by weight and the manufacturer's color name (for example, 100 gram white).

This paper is great for flowers that demand a thinner petal but still require texture and durability. Please note that 100 gram "peach" is somewhat beige, so I refer to it as "peach/beige," and that 100 gram "brown" is quite gray, so it is called out as "brown/gray" throughout the text.

90 gram German "Gloria" doublette crepe

Specified by the supplier's color name and "doublette" (for example, white/white or cream/yellow doublette).

This crepe paper comes in folds rather than rolls. It is made by laminating two layers of different colored lightweight crepe together, hence the name "doublette." I depend on my stockpile of folds of olive green doublette for my favorite leaves, but it comes in many other color combinations, with a smooth texture perfectly suited for flower petals.

60 gram Italian florist crepe

Specified by weight, manufacturer's color number, and a general color name (for example, 60 gram #330 white).

This very thin crepe is a more elusive material in the United States, but it makes beautiful, soft flowers. I use it more for inner elements and color highlights than for full petals, as it is not durable enough for my liking and crumples rather easily. It does have a very natural appearance and comes in a gorgeous color selection. You can create your own doublette crepe by laminating two layers of 60 gram crepe together with tacky glue or spray adhesive.

Crepe party streamers and single-ply folds

Specified by a general color descriptor (for example, white streamers).

I rarely use these items, but they work well for ultra-thin bougainvillea bracts and certain fringes, or when laminated to heavier crepe for unique color combinations.

basic tips for working with crepe paper

Here are some things to keep in mind when making paper flowers with crepe paper.

PAPER GRAIN

The creping texture, or "grain," of the paper is the most important thing to pay attention to when making paper flowers. It is what allows the paper to stretch and what gives it its strength. The petal and leaf templates and guides each have three parallel lines on them indicating grain direction. Those lines should always be oriented in the direction of the paper grain before cutting, whether it be straight up and down for the petals, or at an angle, as is the case for most leaves and bracts. Trace or copy templates onto the (non-crepe) paper of your choice before cutting them out, and always cut your crepe as close to the templates as possible.

Many times, petal strips, individual petals, and fringe are cut from strips of crepe at a certain size, with the vertical dimension of the strip referred to as "tall" and the horizontal dimension referred to as "long." The "tall" dimension will always be the direction of the paper grain, even if it is shorter than the length of the strip.

MACHINE LINES

The 100, 160, and 180 gram rolls of crepe paper have continuous machine lines running perpendicular to the grain, spaced around 1¾" apart. When petal sizes allow, cut them out between the machine lines, or locate the lines at the bottom of the petals. Sometimes they can't be avoided, especially in the giant flowers, but their appearance will soften when the petals are groomed by stretching or cupping.

PAPER WEIGHTS

The heavier the paper, the more it will stretch. Therefore, a flower originally specified in 100 gram paper will become larger and possibly distorted when made with 180 gram paper. Keep this in mind when substituting papers in a tutorial. It will become easier to successfully make adjustments once you get used to working with the crepe.

OUTSTRETCHING

Many of the steps in the tutorials call for the paper to be fully outstretched. *Outstretching* means stretching the crepe of the paper to the point where the paper is more or less completely smooth before using it. This gives the paper a thin, natural look while still maintaining some ability to be shaped. Be aware that any amount of stretching will almost always slightly lighten the color of the crepe.

LAMINATING

Laminating crepe paper is a great way to create a composite piece of crepe by adhering two or more colors together for fringed stamens. It can also allow you more control over the location of different colors on bicolored petals, and is also useful in reinforcing thinner crepe papers.

WEAR AND TEAR, SUNLIGHT, AND MOISTURE

The crepe paper used in this book is durable, and the flowers meant to be worn and enjoyed without kid gloves. However, do be mindful of how and where you store your crepe paper stash to avoid crumpling or crushing, and don't bang your final products around too much. Most of the crepe paper colors, especially the darker and brighter ones, should be kept away from direct sunlight and excessive heat to prevent fading. Some of the papers are water resistant, but, in general, all crepe paper should be kept away from moisture.

OMBRÉ CREPE PAPER

Ombré crepe paper is special. It comes in beautiful and interesting color blends that are applied to only one side of the paper. Ombré paper has been used in several tutorials throughout the book, but can always be replaced with a single color or a combination of colors to mimic the gradated look of ombré petals.

More specific techniques for shaping and grooming crepe paper petals, including some that are mentioned here, are detailed in "Basic Techniques" on page 23.

wire and glue

Here are a few simple notes about working with wire and glue, and a bit about using floral tape for wrapping stems.

WIRE

Every tutorial calls for a specific type of stem wire—chosen for its color, finish, or thickness—but they are somewhat interchangeable since you can always wrap them with floral tape or paper to achieve the effect you want. The thickness of the wire is called out by gauge: the smaller the gauge the thicker the wire. I like to keep thinner cloth-covered wire around for the center ribs of leaves, and lots of thicker cloth-covered and brown paper–wrapped wire on hand for stems, all in 18"-long straight lengths, as opposed to on a spool. Almost every flower requires the top of the stem wire to be bent into a tight hook or loop in which to interlock the beginning of the flower in some way. This prevents the flower heads from popping off the top as you work. Use a pair of wire cutters or pliers and some muscle to bend and close the end of the wire as required.

Waxy floral tape goes hand in hand with stem wire. It is a quick way to attach leaves to stems with a finished look. To use floral tape, simply wrap it around the stem wire while stretching tightly, which will activate the sticky wax embedded in the tape and allow it to adhere to the wire. Floral tape comes in an array of colors, but I use the light- and dark-green and dark-brown tapes most frequently. I also use it to form the bases for buds and pods. To make quicker work of them, let the tape fold over onto itself or even stretch into a thick string while wrapping around the wire, opening back up to smooth the surface out occasionally. This will add more bulk to your bud or pod faster, but remember to wrap as tightly as you can.

GLUE

I use only two types of glue: tacky glue and hot glue applied with a mini glue gun set on low. Tacky glue allows the flower petals to sit closer together in a more natural manner, but hot glue can get things done much quicker and adds durability.

I apply tacky glue three different ways. Most often, I use a small but sturdy paintbrush, but on other occasions I will dab it on straight from the bottle and use my finger to spread and thin it. Other times I will stick my finger into a pool of tacky glue and wipe it onto the petal bases, especially if I want to move quickly. Prepare to have gluey fingers at times. More often than not, you will find me staring into space, holding a flower to dry in one hand while I am rolling the glue off my fingers of the other.

One other thing about tacky glue: it is wet, and in cooler climates if there is too much of it on your continuous petal strips and petal bases, things can turn sideways quickly. I have pointed out in the tutorials where you should let the glue set up a few minutes between steps, but it is generally good to wait a beat whenever you can to ensure your flower adheres together properly.

simple tools & materials & special items

Following is a list of the items besides paper, wire, and glue that I use on a daily basis. They are mostly household items that have made their way into my work through sheer convenience. The scissors I use most often are kitchen scissors, purchased for six dollars at an art supply store. They may not be meant to be used on paper, but I can't work without them. When choosing scissors, select a pair that fits your hand, and be sure it cuts finely enough to fringe paper, as that is an important component of paper flower making.

One of my secret weapons is a thin, 8"-long pointed metal hat pin that my husband gave me years ago. It is perfect for curling petals, applying glue, and separating stamens, and I can't live without it. I recommend finding one, but if you don't have one, you can substitute a piece of 16-gauge stem wire, an upholstery needle, a round-edged toothpick, or a thin bamboo skewer, whenever a hat pin is called for.

Keep an assortment of small, firm-bristled paintbrushes for general purposes, like applying small touches of stain and thin lines of glue. Tiny scissors are a must, for obvious reasons. Wire cutters can be used for cutting, bending, and crimping wire, but use pliers if you are more comfortable bending wire with them.

Most of the coloring and treating of paper is done with chalk, coffee, tea, a little red ink or liquid concentrated watercolor, or stain made by soaking crepe paper in water. (Coloring and treatment is covered in detail in the special technique section on page 51.) Protect surfaces and clothing when treating paper, and use rubbing alcohol to help remove stains from your fingers if necessary.

Find sources for select items on pages 16 and 17.

SIMPLE TOOLS & MATERIALS
These items are used throughout the tutorials.

Assorted paintbrushes	Rubbing alcohol
Black coffee and tea	Ruler
Crimson liquid concentrated watercolor (such as Dr. Ph. Martin's)	Sidewalk chalk
	Thin bamboo skewers
Hat pin or similar curling implement	Tiny scissors
	Toothpicks
Paper cutting scissors of your choice	Water
	Wire cutters
Pliers	
Red writing ink	

SPECIAL ITEMS
Some of the tutorials contain one or more of these "special" everyday items, many of which are optional. Additional items for the wearables in chapter 4 and the giant paper peony in chapter 5 can be found in those tutorials.

Alpine Rose and Mahogany liquid concentrated watercolor	Rounded, pointed medium-size paintbrush
Black India ink	Sharp graphite pencil
Bleach	Small glass bowls
Blending brush	Spoon
Butter knife	Tiny paintbrush for details
Chicken's eggs, or paper-covered plastic or papier-mâché eggs	Unscented cosmetic pink-mauve blush
Extra-sharp scissors	Upholstery needles
Gold metallic eye shadow	Waxed paper
Kitchen sponge	White cloth-covered stem wire
Kitchen towel	Wide, firm paintbrush for spreading lots of glue
Mod Podge	Wide, soft paintbrush for applying swaths of color
Parchment paper	Wooden disposable chopsticks with rounded edges
Protective gloves	
Rolling pin	

sources

These are my favorite places to find and order crepe paper, wire, and floral tape, followed by some additional sellers and sources for select special and sundry items found in this book. Common craft supplies such as glue, scissors, paintbrushes, Mod Podge, bamboo skewers, sidewalk chalk, and other simple materials can be found at your local craft, grocery, or hardware stores.

CARTE FINI FINE ITALIAN PAPERS
www.cartefini.com
1.888.284.6532

- 180 gram Italian florist crepe paper in solid and ombré (or nuanced) colors
- 60 gram Italian crepe paper

CASTLE IN THE AIR
www.castleintheair.biz
1.510.204.9801

- 160 and 180 gram German and Italian florist crepe paper
- 90 gram German "Gloria" doublette crepe paper
- Select cloth-covered stem wire segments

D. BLÜMCHEN & COMPANY
www.blumchen.com
1.866.653.9627

- 90 gram German "Gloria" doublette crepe paper
- Single-ply crepe paper folds

DICK BLICK ART MATERIALS
www.dickblick.com
1.800.828.4548

- Dr. Ph. Martin's radiant liquid concentrated watercolors

ETSY
www.etsy.com

- Vintage hat pins (for use as tools), any length
- Skinny, fabric-wrapped elastic headbands

www.etsy.com/shop/fancygoods
- Hat elastics

www.etsy.com/shop/LushLapel
- Teardrop-shaped 4"-wide by 7"-long sinamay fascinator bases

MISTER ART
www.misterart.com
1.800.721.3015

- Single-ply crepe paper folds and streamers

PAPER MART
www.papermart.com
1.800.745.8800

- 100 and 180 gram Chinese crepe paper
- Green and white cloth-covered 18" stem wire (all gauges)
- Brown paper–wrapped 18" stem wire (18 gauge)
- Thin, uncovered green 18" stem wire (24 gauge)
- Light- and dark-green and dark-brown floral tape

SAVE-ON-CRAFTS
www.save-on-crafts.com
1.831.768.8428

- Select cloth-covered and brown paper–wrapped 18" stem wire
- Light- and dark-green and dark-brown floral tape

32° NORTH
www.vintage-ornaments.com
1.760.487.8580

- 90 gram German "Gloria" doublette crepe paper

If you cannot find the following supplies at your local art and craft stores, most can be ordered through online sellers like Amazon.

- Assorted stem wire segments and other supplies (including my favorite brand of floral tape for both color and usability, Floratape)
- Clauss 3" titanium fine-cut "tiny" scissors
- Crepe paper streamers in special colors like peach and coral
- Dr. Ph. Martin's radiant liquid concentrated watercolors
- Embroidery thread
- Paper-covered plastic or papier-mâché eggs

CHAPTER 2

the flowers

BASIC TECHNIQUES & STARTER SPECIMENS

These flowers are made using a range of basic techniques. Some, like the bougainvillea, I have been making since I first discovered my love of paper flowers, and I enjoy seeing how much they have evolved since my first attempts. Each of the five starter specimens included here grows in a wide range of colors, so it is possible to use the same paper color and type for more than one of these tutorials. The basic techniques used here will be used throughout this book and will help you create beautiful and convincing versions of these flowers at any skill level.

CUTTING

CURLING

CUPPING & STRETCHING

RUFFLING & RIPPLING

FRINGING

OUTSTRETCHING

CRUSHING, CRUMPLING & SPINDLING

LAMINATING

basic techniques

It is especially important to me to never leave the crepe untouched in order to give it movement and life. These eight basic but nuanced techniques help in creating the most lifelike botanical specimens possible.

CUTTING

Cut through no more than four layers of crepe paper at a time for accuracy. Orient your templates properly atop the paper and cut closely around them. Guides are provided in some cases to indicate the size and shape of certain fringes, petal strips, and petals. Compare your work with the guides, but don't attempt to cut around the components on a guide by using it as a template.

CUPPING & STRETCHING

Cupping is a technique that I use frequently, usually to create a concave petal face. Using both hands, hold your petal facing you between your thumbs and forefingers. Press your thumbs deeply into the center of the paper while pulling the backside outward with your forefingers, leaving the edges unstretched. Do not be afraid to cup your petals deeply to insure the proper form of your flower.

To stretch a petal, gently pull outward while holding along its top edge to widen the petal edge or thin the paper as needed.

FRINGING

Fringing is one of my strong suits, and I assure you that the more you practice it, the easier it will be. Fringing is so important to my paper flower making that it has its own section at the beginning of "Fringe-Centered Flowers" (see page 87).

CRUSHING, CRUMPLING & SPINDLING

To crush a petal, roll the paper back around a skewer or hat pin, then squash it together while still rolled around the tool. To crumple paper, simply wad it into a tight ball. To spindle paper, gather toward the petal or strip's centerline and twist one way, then the other, then unfurl.

CURLING

Rolling the top or sides of a petal back around a skewer or hat pin gives them a natural curl.

RUFFLING & RIPPLING

Pinch the top edge of your petal or paper between your thumbnail and the pad or nail of your forefinger and pull in quick, short movements perpendicular to the grain, as you would do to curl ribbon against scissors.

OUTSTRETCHING

Outstretching is used to turn thick, textured paper into thin, smooth paper that can still be cupped and shaped. Hold each end of a strip of paper and rub it back and forth forcefully across your thigh or the edge of a table until it is taut and smooth. Crepe paper is less delicate than you would think, so don't be afraid to give it a good stretch. Work with strips that are around 2" tall for uniform stretching.

LAMINATING

Laminating together two or more layers of crepe paper with tacky glue is simple. Spread a thin consistent layer of glue on the face of one strip of paper, lay a second strip of paper on top with the grain in the same direction, and rub in the direction of the grain to adhere.

bougainvillea

Tacky glue

Hot glue

180 gram #572 magenta crepe paper

180 gram #588 deep maroon crepe paper

180 gram #600 white crepe paper

Light-green floral tape

24-gauge green floral wire

Leaves (see page 194)

Bougainvillea is known in some parts of the world as the "paper flower" and I can see why—it translates so beautifully in paper. Growing up in New Hampshire, I am not sure I ever came across a bougainvillea vine, but it is abundant here in San Francisco, growing in massive clusters in nearly every neighborhood. The colorful parts of the bougainvillea plant are actually called bracts, not petals. The bracts are structured similarly to many leaves, each with two sides connecting along a center rib. The flowers are tiny blossoms at the tips of the bougainvillea's three central buds. I don't often add these little flowers to my paper bougainvillea, as they are a bit fussy and not always present on the plant itself, but I have included them in the tutorial, and they do look nice when added.

The color selection for bougainvillea is large. I've used a magenta crepe paper in this tutorial, but bougainvillea is equally as beautiful in shades of yellow, red, purple, maroon, coral, and even white. I like to use outstretched heavy crepe paper for its durability and texture, but peach or coral crepe paper streamers are a gorgeous alternative, especially if washed with a light maroon stain (see page 55). A small cluster of bougainvillea tucked behind your ear is lovely, a giant headdress of them magnificent. See more in chapter 4 "Things to Wear & Things for Your Hair."

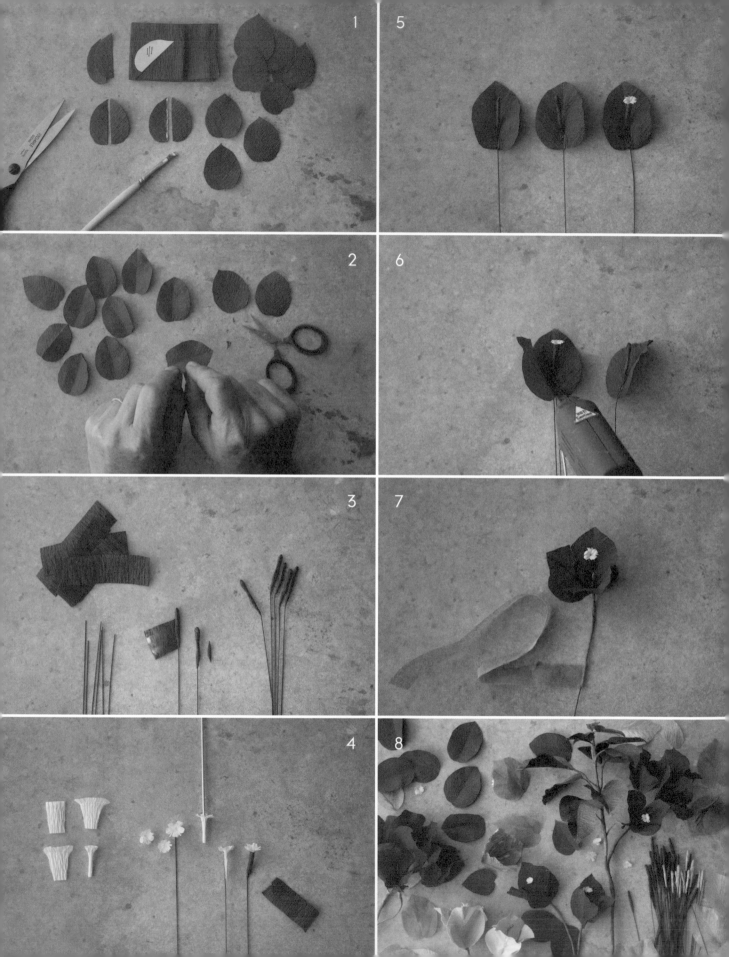

1 For the bracts, outstretch a 2"-tall by 5"-long strip of 180 gram #572 magenta crepe paper. Fold the strip onto itself six times, orient your desired template size B1 to B5 at an angle on top of the paper with the three parallel lines matching the grain, and cut six bract halves. Apply a thin line of tacky glue down the edge of one of the halves. Place the edge of an opposing half over the glued edge and press gently between your thumb and forefinger to create a full bract, the grain pointing up and out from the center rib. Check that the two sides overlap no more than $\frac{1}{16}$" by holding up to a light source; decrease the overlap if necessary by pulling the sides outward to slide apart. Repeat with the other halves to create three completed bracts.

2 Trim the tips of each bract and crease each inward along its centerline. Ripple the top edges of each between your thumbnail and finger with the bract facing you, then repeat at the bottom with the bract facing away. Vary the ripples a bit so the bracts are not totally uniform.

3 To create simple buds, cut three $\frac{3}{8}$"-tall by 2"-long strips of outstretched 180 gram #588 deep maroon crepe paper and three 6"-long segments of 24-gauge floral wire. Roll one strip of paper snugly around the top of a wire and secure with light tacky glue, rounding the top as you go. Pinch the center tightly to form a $\frac{3}{4}$"-long hourglass-shaped bud with a slightly bulbous tip and tapered bottom, snipping away small slivers from the side of the bud, if necessary, to accentuate the shape. Reroll to seal. Repeat with the remaining paper strips and wires. Bend each bud slightly, about 5 degrees, just below the taper.

4 To create optional tiny blossoms, use template B6 to cut a trapezoid from a piece of 180 gram #600 white crepe paper, with the $\frac{1}{8}$"-tall machining rib along the top edge if possible. Gently ripple the top edge and bend the top

$\frac{1}{8}$" back. Trim away the top overstretched corners, apply light tacky glue below the bend, and roll the trapezoid onto itself tightly. Flair open the top $\frac{1}{8}$" and glue the open edge together with a minuscule overlap. Cut five evenly spaced $\frac{3}{32}$"-deep slits around the rim, then another five just a hair from the first. Round the corners of each petal with tiny scissors. Open up the very center a bit by inserting a hat pin, then lightly hot glue the side of the blossom to the end of a piece of floral wire. Wrap with a small segment of outstretched maroon crepe just below the petals, and bend the wire very slightly, about 5 degrees, just below the taper.

5 Set the $\frac{1}{4}$" of wire just below your buds or blossoms in small beads of hot glue at the bases of the three bracts, so that the bottom of each bud or blossom sits $\frac{1}{4}$" above the bottom of the bracts, angled away from the bract faces.

6 Apply a small drop of hot glue just to the right of the bud on the bottom face of one of the bracts. Immediately press the face of a second bract directly opposite the first, before the glue cools. Open the bracts back up and add a small bead of hot glue at their bases where they meet, then quickly press the bottom center of the third bract into that spot.

7 Bend the bud bases to open the bracts as desired, curving the bud tips slightly toward the center. Wrap the bud wires together with floral tape, or thin the stem by clipping one bud wire off completely, 2" off another, and leaving one full length before wrapping to one or two other clusters, about $1\frac{3}{4}$" below the bracts.

8 Preparing bracts and buds in bulk can make quick work of large bougainvillea clusters. Attach two single leaves or large leafy vines, and have fun playing with different crepe paper and streamer colors.

carnation

Tacky glue

Hot glue

180 gram peach/beige crepe paper, the end dipped in stain made from maroon crepe (see page 54) or candy striped Pattern 1 (see page 114)

100 gram moss green crepe paper

180 gram #566 pale green or other light colored crepe paper

Lemon-yellow sidewalk chalk

Light-green floral tape

16-gauge green cloth-covered stem wire

Leaves (see page 194)

In the United States, carnations might be the most underrated and unappreciated of flowers, relegated to prom corsages and grocery-store bouquets. But for those of us in the know, they are the sleeper stars of modern floristry and centuries-old works of art alike. This somewhat botanically correct version of the carnation comes together quickly into a form that is instantly recognizable. Make them from cream-colored crepe with a tinge of green tea or peach/beige paper with an irregular stain of berry-red dye for an antique carnation look. And, of course, try the candy-striped carnation, whose variations are found as frequently as the morning glory in the paintings of the Dutch masters. Zigzagging, or "pinking," the edges of the petals with tiny scissors when making candy-striped carnations will put them completely over the top.

A few notes on the construction: Use tacky glue when it cooperates and attaches petals easily, switching to hot glue whenever needed to keep the petals in the correct position. Petals should be connected to the stem only at the base, allowing other petals to be slid in between them all the way to the center. For a simpler calyx, cut shapes CC1 and CC2 from outstretched green crepe paper and wrap around the base of the flower, CC2 covering where the calyx meets the stem. Templates C3 and C4 can be used to make a smaller carnation.

1 Cut 24 type C1 petals from 3"-tall strips of 180 gram crepe in your choice of color that have been stretched as far as you can stretch them between your hands easily without forcing. This will leave a tiny amount of crepe in the paper to give it some movement, as opposed to completely outstretching it. Stretch the top of each petal between your thumbnail and forefinger on either side of the V from the center outward, then run your thumb up the center of each from base to tip to crease.

2 Run your thumbnail up the face of each petal again, this time using the width of the nail to stretch a wide furrow in the petal, stopping ½" from the top. Using your fingertip (or a paintbrush), apply tacky glue to the bottom of each petal and gather by folding one side in, then the other. Press the petals open just above the glued area to be sure they don't close up on themselves.

3 Create loose stacks of the petals and glue each together at the base. You will need six stacks of three, two stacks of two folded onto themselves, and two individual petals glued together side by side. Use hot glue to attach the side of the base of one stack of three petals to the top ½" of the stem wire.

4 Attach three more stacks of three petals to the top of the stem with hot glue per step 3, spacing the four stacks evenly around the flower. When viewed from the top, they should create two C shapes, back to back. Attach the two side-by-side C1 petals spine out at the 12 o'clock position, and a set of two stacked and folded petals, also spine out, at the 9 o'clock position.

5 Cut 32 type C2 petals from 3½"-tall strips of crepe that have been stretched similarly to step 1. Pull the top of each petal lightly between your thumbnail and forefinger on either side of the V, from the center outward, to create just a hint of a ripple. Gather the bottom ¾" of each base with tacky glue. Set 18 of the petals aside for use in steps 8 to 10, and cup the bellies of the rest on each side of the V. Cup deeply so the tops begin to curl up and over.

6 Fit the first seven of the cupped type C2 petals around the flower, sliding them in between the stacked smaller petals. Slide their edges in so they meet at or near the middle of the flower in the positions listed in the next paragraph. Set each one ¹⁄₁₆" above the smaller petals, cupping slightly over, with their tops all aligned. If you press too tightly at the base, it will pull the petals back out from the center. Use a little tacky glue along the edges toward the center to keep them in place, then anchor the floating bases below with tacky glue, or hot glue when needed. Carefully gather the bases in before the glue sets all the way when you can.

Locate the C2 petals at the following positions: 1, 3, 5, 6, 9, 11 o'clock, and a folded C2 with the spine side out cupping around the smaller petals in the 8 to 9 o'clock region. This is not an exact science, but will get you close to a nice facsimile of a carnation.

7 Fold two cupped C2 petals outward into V shapes. Slide one, crease side in, at 12 o'clock and the other at 6. Fold one on itself and slide between the C2 petals at 5 and 6 o'clock. Fold another on itself, then glue a set of two folded smaller petals inside it with their spines out. Slide this in at the 3 to 4 o'clock position, with the larger petal's crease toward the center of the flower. Use the final two sets of three and one set of two smaller petals to fill in around the flower at your discretion. They do not need to touch the center of the flower, but should be placed snugly within the folds.

8 The final three cupped C2 petals help soften the transition between the upright center petals and the outer, more horizontal ones. Bend each base back 1½" from the tops, add hot glue along the top of the bend, and slide into gaps or spiral with other C2 petals where it looks natural, attaching them 1¼" to 1½" down from the top of the flower. They should be somewhat diagonal, the edges of the petal toward the center more upright, the outer edges swirling down.

CONTINUED

9 Groom the remaining 18 C2 petals with your thumbnail per step 2 and stretch slightly to widen, or leave unstretched for a more compact flower. Fold the petals back at their halfway points and attach three with hot glue along the bends, just below the three petals from step 8. Pinch the bent areas down to ¼" to ⅜" wide if needed to assist attachment.

10 The rest of the petals should be attached near the same level as the petals in step 9, using tacky glue, or hot glue for extra hold when needed. Stagger them over and under each other, some at a slight diagonal, others warped up or down, avoiding striation. Let three petals dangle down at their sides while sliding their center lines upwards at 45-degree angles between their other petals. The bottommost petals should be horizontal or angled slightly downward.

11 Carefully snip away excess hot glue at the base, slimming to ½" to ¾" diameter at the top. Inject hot glue into any voids in the base and squeeze carefully to compact. Brush tacky glue behind the petal bases and smooth down to taper. Laminate five pieces of light-green floral tape to a 2"-high piece of completely outstretched moss green crepe paper in the grain direction. Cut out the strips, shaping a wide point at the end of each. Crease their center lines to add dimension, then tacky glue them around the base evenly, with the top ⅛" of each strip unglued, leaving no gaps between the strips. The tips should just touch the underside of the petals. Cut away any excess and smooth down. Cut shape CC2 from the outstretched green paper, dust with lemon-yellow chalk, and wrap around the base where it meets the stem, leaving the top ⅛" unglued. Wrap the stem with floral tape, attaching leaves as described on page 194, or leave bare.

12 For the stigma, cut three 1¼"-tall string-like strips with the grain of the paper from outstretched pale green crepe. Wipe lightly with tacky glue and roll between fingers to round, then curl the pointed tops around a paintbrush. Set into the nooks near the center of the flower using a bit of glue at the ends, the curls popping out the top just a bit.

daffodil & double daffodil

Tacky glue

Hot glue

White and light yellow/
yellow doublette crepe
paper (petals and
coronas)

Orange/red orange,
light salmon/light rose,
and pale pink/apricot
doublette crepe paper
(additional corona and
stain colors)

100 gram gold
crepe paper

180 gram #566 pale green
crepe paper

100 gram brown/gray
crepe paper (spathe)

Water

Crimson liquid
concentrated watercolor

Small glass bowls

Round, pointed
paintbrush

Tiny paintbrush

Bamboo skewers,
1 per flower

Dark-green floral tape

20-gauge green
cloth-covered stem wire

Leaves (page 194)

Wooden disposable
chopsticks with rounded
edges, 1 per flower
(optional)

A daffodil is a narcissus and a narcissus is a daffodil. It took me a while to understand that they are synonymous, but now that I know, I am happy to be able to freely use the word *daffodil* when referring to these flowers.

Paper daffodils are a delight. While you can't go wrong with an all-yellow or all-white daffodil, experimenting with color combinations is half the fun. I have included double daffodils because they are gorgeous and just rare enough around most parts that if you put them together "wrong," no one will notice.

I use doublette crepe paper due to its spot-on color selection and texture. Instead of using a rippling technique at the corona, I like to use small cuts and water or stain to bend the edges back and give the illusion of a continuous, natural ruffle. Make a few more coronas than you need, as working with water can be unpredictable sometimes, for better or worse. Undiluted red liquid concentrated watercolor applied lightly to the top edges of a corona with a tiny paintbrush after bending them with moisture can really make them glow.

Bamboo skewers are used for the stalks, but for a thicker appearance you can add a rounded wooden chopstick as shown in the Double Daffodil tutorial. In lieu of the brown crepe specified for the spathe, feel free to substitute crumpled brown parchment paper.

DAFFODIL

1 Cut a corona piece in the color and size of your choice using small template D1, medium D2, or large D3. Accordion fold the longer top edge of the trapezoid tightly, stretching the paper away from you after each fold. Make ⅛"-deep rounded cuts in the top edge as shown on the corona templates. Spindle below the accordioned folds, then open and apply tacky glue down one edge of the trapezoid. Wrap around your finger (or a pencil) and press down to seal, holding the seam closed with your thumb. Gather the base end closed with glue, twisting to form either a point or a rounded end molded around the tip of your finger, adjusting to your desired corona length. Trim where the paper is higher at the seam, so it is level with the rest of the corona.

2 Use either plain water or stain to ruffle the corona. If using stain, soak one 2" square of orange/red orange, light salmon/light rose, or light yellow/yellow doublette in 1½ tablespoons of water for about 1 minute in a small glass bowl. Dip a round, pointed paintbrush in plain water or the stain, remove excess moisture from the belly of the brush, and lightly pat around the top edge of the corona. Bend the edge back with the brush as the paper softens. Deepen the color if desired by lightly dabbing the wet edge with a red stain made from 3 drops of liquid concentrated watercolor mixed in 1 tablespoon water. Set the corona down on its top edge to dry, pinching the edges gently after 10 minutes to create a more rippled appearance. Let sit for 10 minutes longer, then pinch gently again before fully dry.

3 Make a quick rendition of the anthers by tightly wrapping a ¼"-tall by 3"-long outstretched strip of 100 gram gold crepe paper with tacky glue around the end of a piece of 20-gauge green cloth-covered stem wire, extending ⅜" past the end of the wire. Make ³⁄₁₆"-deep snips with tiny scissors into the end to create five little points and bend them outward into a tiny star. Trim the gathered corona base to ⅜"-long, snip a tiny hole at the bottom next to the base, and thread the stem wire through, locating the inner star ¼" to ⅜" down from the top. Glue the wire along the base.

4 Cut out six type D4, D5, or D6 petals in your desired size and color. Crease the centerline of each petal, spindle tightly, then gently open back up. Crimp the base with glue and bend back the bottom ¾" to 1" of each. For all petal sizes, pinch the petal tips together with a hint of glue, trim if needed, and roll the top edges inward along a hat pin. The smallest D4 petals can be stretched lightly across their bellies to open them up a bit. The larger D5 and D6 petals can be fashioned naturally by running your thumbnail up the back or front centerlines or creating a ¹⁄₁₆" permanent crease in the backs of some with a light skim of glue.

5 Tacky glue the petal bases at any point along the bottom third of the corona, smoothing down to taper, and pressing from the inside with a skewer to help adhere. Space the first three evenly around the flower with gaps in between them, then fill the gaps with the second three petals between or just below the first. Each petal should be the same width where it touches the corona. Glue a strip of ⅝"-tall outstretched pale green crepe paper with a ripped top edge just below the petals.

6 Attach a bamboo skewer to the wire stem 1¾" down from the bottom of the petals with dark-green floral tape, wrapping tightly from the top of the skewer down, keeping the wire straight. Wrap tape around the stem at the bottom of the pale-green paper until it becomes a bulbous shape resembling the ovary, about ¼" long and a little wider than the base of the flower where it sits. Continue down to cover any exposed wire.

7 Cut the spathe from outstretched 100 gram brown/gray crepe using template D7 or D8. Spindle, open, and glue the bottom ½" neatly around the stem just below the top of the skewer, overlapping, with the opening facing up or down. Bend the stem down 45 degrees above the skewer, then very slightly, another 5 degrees, below the ovary.

8 Experiment with size and colors. See the Double Daffodil (page 38) for tips on thickening the stalk.

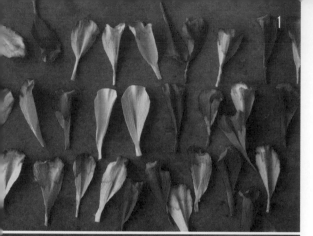

DOUBLE DAFFODIL

1 Cut five D9 and eighteen D10 corona pieces from the doublette crepe color of your choice. Gather each at the base with tacky glue, then ruffle the top edges with your thumbnail. Bend the top edges back with water or stain to ruffle per step 2 of the Daffodil tutorial (page 36). Set aside to dry.

2 Cut five small D11, six medium D4, and twelve large D5 petals from white or yellow doublette and cup each one. Randomly curl the top edges of the five D11 petals inward or backward over a hat pin, crushing and then reopening a few while curling. Nest four D9 corona pieces ⅜" down inside four D11 petals with tacky glue at their bases. Make a small hook at the top of the stem wire and hot glue the side of the base of one nested petal to the wire, followed by the freestanding D9 corona piece perpendicular to that. Glue one free-standing D11 petal and the three other petal sets with coronas inward around the center in a random swirl, their tops sitting ⅛" down from the central top petal.

3 Curl the top edges of the six D4 petals inward, crushing and then smoothing a few. Tacky glue six D10 corona pieces ½" down inside the petals, then glue them around the flower, staggered just below the first row. Crease the twelve D5 petals up their back centerlines with your thumbnail, shape their tips per template D5, then crease the front faces diagonally with your thumbnail ⅛" in from each side, forcing the outer edges to fold inward slightly. Glue six D10 corona pieces low in six of the petals in such a way that the petals will protrude ¼" farther than the row above, while the corona pieces will be aligned with those above. Attach with tacky glue, concentrating less on staggering the petals evenly and more on getting a well-rounded flower.

4 Repeat the end of step 3 with the last six petals and corona pieces, keeping both at the same distance from the center as the previous row, rounding out the flower as needed. Finish per steps 5 to 7 from the Daffodil tutorial (page 37). To thicken the stalk further, wrap a rounded wooden chopstick next to the stalk with floral tape before attaching the spathe.

japanese form peony

Tacky glue

Hot glue

180 gram #603 cream crepe paper

100 gram yellow crepe paper (optional)

White doublette crepe paper

60 gram #212 magenta crepe paper, or 180 gram #572 magenta crepe paper (optional)

Olive green (or other green of your choice) doublette crepe paper

Crimson liquid concentrated watercolor

Tiny paintbrush

Wide, firm paintbrush (optional)

16-gauge green cloth-covered stem wire

Leaves (see page 195)

Mod Podge (optional)

Selecting the peonies for this book was so difficult that I ended up including three different types. The first and simplest of the three is the Japanese form peony, which typically has a few rows of larger outer petals surrounding a fluffy center cluster of smaller, pointed petals, or petaloids, and is somewhat flatter in profile than other types of peonies. This tutorial is specifically for the Bride's Dream peony, whose white outer petals are similar to those of the Honey Gold and Primevere peonies, among others. Also included are optional colors and instructions for the Bowl of Beauty peony, which requires only a small change of petal technique and colors. The petals of the Bowl of Beauty can range from lavender-purple to hot pink, so I've settled on magenta paper for this tutorial.

The Japanese form peony is fun to play with, and won't look entirely unnatural if you mix and match colors or make the entire thing deep burgundy.

Although you can make the petals on these peonies perfectly cupped, I prefer to groom the petals in slightly different ways to avoid a uniform look. Mod Podge is applied to the paper before cutting and shaping the outer petals on the Bowl of Beauty to give it interesting sheen and shape and to strengthenthe thinner crepe. Be sure to leave time for the Mod Podge to dry, if using.

1 For a Bride's Dream, cut three 2"-tall by 18"-long JP6 continuous petal strips from outstretched 180 gram #603 cream crepe paper. Cut the vertical slits first, then all the corners in one direction. Flip the paper over and cut the opposite corners, then finish by cutting the center slits. Spindle each strip firmly.

For a Bowl of Beauty, cut three 2¼"-tall by 18"-long JP7 strips from outstretched 100 gram yellow crepe in the same manner. Spindle only the tips and bottoms, leaving the center section uncrumpled for wider petaloids.

2 Bend the top of the stem wire into a tight ⅜"-tall M shape. Interlock the end of a petal strip with the wire, the top of the petals 1" above the top of the M. Wrap each strip tightly around the wire with a light layer of tacky glue along the bottom, keeping the bottoms level. Squeeze the base together and upward to flatten and minimize bulk as much as possible. For the Bride's Dream, add the suggestion of anthers by carefully dabbing crimson liquid concentrated watercolor onto the top of the stem wire M deep in the center of the cream petaloids with a tiny paintbrush.

3 For the Bride's Dream, cut two JP1, three JP2, four JP3, and three JP4 petals from white doublette. Cup the widest part of each petal into a ½"-deep round bowl, not too curved in at the sides like a channel, which can sometimes happen. Gather the bottom ¾" of each with tacky glue, pleating the left side over the right like a Z. Bend the JP1 and JP2 bases back ½", the JP3 and JP4 back ¾". Lightly stretch the two top edges of the split-topped JP1 and JP3 petals, creasing or folding one JP1 and one JP3 upward along its centerline, forcing the sides to drape downward a bit. Very lightly stretch the top edges of the JP2 and JP4 petals so they're thinned and lightly undulating, but not frilly. Trim any edges of the petals that might've become too wide or distorted by cupping or grooming.

For a Bowl of Beauty, use a wide, firm paintbrush to apply a thin coat of Mod Podge on both sides of two 10" square pieces of 60 gram or 180 gram magenta crepe. Hang to dry overnight. When dry, cut 9 or 10 type JP5 petals, then cup and stretch each until around 2"-wide at the centers. Gather the bottom 1½" of each petal base by folding it onto itself with tacky glue, then fold each base back 1½". Leave half of the petals deeply cupped, and groom the other half to be flatter and wrinkled or slightly convex at their centers, with their top edges still scooping upward. Cut a ½"-deep, ⅛"-wide rounded V in the top edge of one or two petals.

4 To attach the petals, apply a ⅜" diameter bead of hot glue to the top face of each petal just above the bend and adhere to the underside of the peony center, touching the bend to the stem and concealing any bulk at the base of the flower. For the Bride's Dream, attach the J1 and J2 petals around the center in an irregular pattern, then glue the J3 and J4 petals staggered in a second row, with a few nested directly behind the inner petals. Bend one of the outer petals downward a bit for a natural look. Trim away the unglued petal bases where they meet the stem, and smooth the cut area down with tacky glue, keeping the base of the flower as flat and bulk-free as possible.

Attach and trim the Bowl of Beauty petals similarly, placing more cupped petals on one half of the flower and flatter ones on the other, giving it the appearance of falling open.

To finish, neatly wrap the stem with ¼"-wide strips of outstretched green crepe, or leave bare, if preferred. For more detail at the base of the flower, see the Faded Coral Charm Peony tutorial on page 169. Bring your peonies even more to life with the addition of a few leaves.

morning glory

Tacky glue

Hot glue

180 gram peacock blue crepe paper (also shown 100 gram iris blue, 180 gram #555 deep blue, and #600/2 sky blue ombré)

100 gram white crepe paper

60 gram #296 yellow crepe paper (optional)

Rounded paintbrush handle

Light-green floral tape

24-gauge green cloth-covered stem wire

Leaves (see page 195)

Bleach (optional)

Small glass bowl (optional)

Round, pointed paintbrush that can be bleached (optional)

In the first incarnation of my botanical art career, I spent countless hours working on detailed watercolor paintings of blue-hued hydrangeas and delphiniums. I revisited those flowers several times when considering which blue flowers I might like to make out of paper, but their tiny petals and parts do not easily lend themselves to three-dimensional work. I was inspired to create morning glories out of paper after noticing their little blue faces poking out of the vases in the still life paintings of the seventeenth-century Dutch and Flemish painters Jan van Huysum, Jan Davidsz. de Heem, and Nicolaes van Verendael, among others. It is a plant-choking nuisance of a weed to some people, so perhaps it represented suffocation or persistence in those works.

Morning glories can be made from virtually any shade of blue crepe paper and still look natural, which I've demonstrated with a few colors here. Their trumpet-like shapes can be made either more realistic or more ethereal by draining the color from the tapered coronas with a little bleach. Instead of a pistil and five stamens, I've taken liberties and just added a few bits of paper-wrapped wire to the centers. This is not the most precise or accurate flower in my arsenal, by any stretch, but it is quick and fun. Try it in shades of red, pink, purple, and white or the candy-striped Carnevale di Venezia Pattern 5 (see page 114).

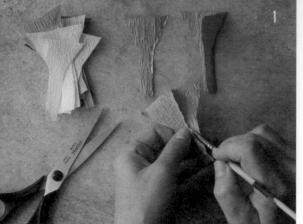

1 Cut five petal segments using template MG from outstretched blue crepe paper in your desired hue. Attach two segments together face-to-face with a line of tacky glue along one edge, starting a hair wider than ¹⁄₁₆" at the base and tapering to a very thin line at the top. Press together to set, then gently open the petals, turn them over and glue the back flap down from the bend in the petal to the base. Repeat with the remaining petal segments, gluing the flaps down in the same direction each time.

2 Crease the centerline of each petal segment inward, then repeat step 1 with the two unattached ends to close the flower and glue the back flap down. Insert a round-ended paintbrush and twist the bottom tip closed below the end. Groom the top open by bending the petals back at each seam gently.

3 Trim the seam corners to round the top of the flower. Cut tiny Vs with rounded edges where the petal segments meet and at their centers. If bleaching, dip a round, pointed paintbrush in a small glass bowl of bleach, wipe off the excess, and insert into the flower's base, bleaching the bottom. Carefully extract the brush, then run the tip up the center of the back of each petal segment to ¾" below the top edge. Allow to dry. Be sure to work in a well-ventilated area. For a tricolored flower, glue small segments of finely fringed outstretched white crepe paper layered with ripped bits of thin yellow crepe paper to the inner petal surfaces before closing.

4 Wrap the top 1½" of two 2"- and one 8"-long pieces of stem wire with outstretched white crepe. Wrap the wires together with floral tape, the 2" pieces set ¾" below the 8" piece, leaving most of the white exposed. Snip the twisted bottom end from the flower and thread the wrapped wire through, aligning the tip of the wires with the bend in the petals. Secure in place with hot glue. Cut five continuous sepal points from a ⅝"-long bit of floral tape and attach at the base of the flower with tacky glue, holding in place until set. Wrap leaf and flower wires around a ¼" paintbrush handle 3 or 4 times in a few different spots to mimic the morning glory's spiraling vines.

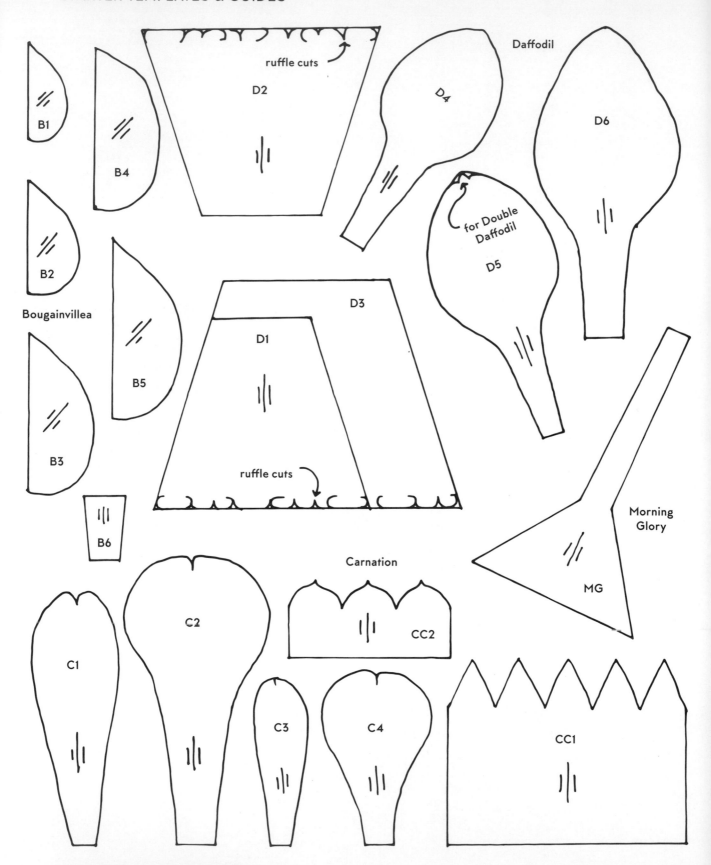

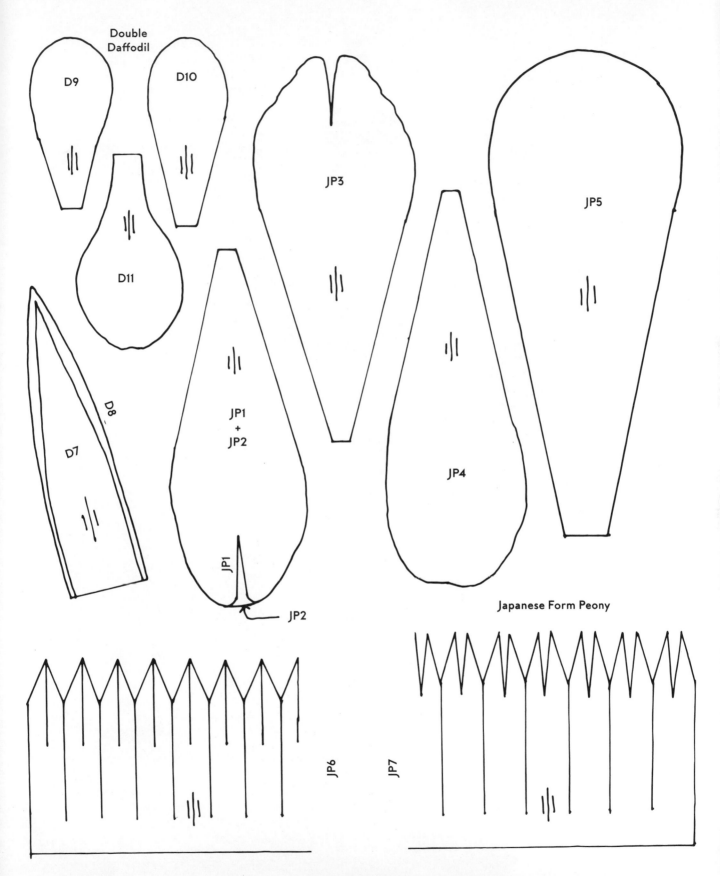

Double
Daffodil

D9

D10

D11

D8

D7

JP1
+
JP2

JP1

JP2

JP3

JP4

JP5

JP6

JP7

Japanese Form Peony

coffee, ink & staining paper with paper

Most of the flowers in this book can be made with crepe paper straight off the roll, and in general, the paper treatments in the tutorials can be taken as suggestions, not necessities. Aside from the occasional dusting of chalk or a brushstroke from my coffee cup, my personal work is most often done with the paper as it comes from the manufacturer. This is partially an attempt to create less work for myself, which is easy because the range of available crepe colors is so great already.

That said, coloring and discoloring your paper can give stunning effects, and it is necessary in some cases, as with wilted and decayed specimens or with flowers that read much truer to life with nuanced petals, like several of the poppies. It is my preference to stain or treat the paper before cutting out the petals. It looks more natural to me to let the chips fall where they may, although sometimes applying color after the fact is the only way to get the job done. I love to color my crepe paper by creating stains from the dyes found in the crepe paper itself. I stumbled upon this by happy accident with some damp crepe a few years ago, and now it is the primary way I color my petals. Drying time for wet crepe paper can vary. If you can hang your paper outdoors on a warm day it will dry within hours; indoors can take longer, sometimes overnight.

Wetting crepe paper will change its texture by breaking down some of the crepe, but in most cases, you can still cup and shape the paper any way you'd like once it's dry. The following pages describe my favorite methods to treat paper. Use them to invent your own special effects in your work. And be sure to wear protective gloves if you are worried about staining your hands while handling these beautiful little messes.

COFFEE AND TEA

Coffee and black tea give the most beautiful tones to some papers. They can subtly deepen corals and reds, and when applied to lighter colored paper they match some of the exact same browns you would see on a fading bloom. Because of its strong smell, I only use coffee for little details, like to darken the edge of a flower or wither a leaf or calyx a bit. Tea can be used full strength and is lighter in color than coffee and without a lingering odor. If you are treating a good amount of crepe paper with tea, brew eight or so tea bags in 4 cups of water and let it cool before using. I like to use a large paintbrush to wash black tea over swaths of white crepe to give it an off-white or aged appearance. I keep some tea-stained crepe paper around at all times to use in both my smaller flowers and my large fine art pieces.

INK AND WATERCOLOR

Ink and liquid concentrated watercolor can be used interchangeably. Keep a bottle of either red India ink or crimson liquid concentrated watercolor on your worktable and use it on lots of things. When used full strength, it can be brushed lightly onto green leaves and stems to give them a more natural appearance, and it is also great for giving a rosy glow to the rim of a daffodil corona. It can be diluted with water or coffee to create a red stain, which deeper-colored paper can be dipped in or painted with to give it more radiance. More shades of ink and watercolor are used in "Candy Striping & Flecking" (page 112).

CHALK

I have two children who love to draw with chalk, and we always have some around, which is why I started using it. Yellow and green sidewalk chalk can be rubbed into petals near a flower's center with a blending brush for natural color gradation or to give the appearance of fallen pollen. I also use yellow chalk to polish the floral tape on the stems of flowers, like dandelions, that require a waxy glow. White chalk can be used on leaves and darker petals for highlights, and pink chalk is a real winner when rubbed into the curled edges of a peach or beige rose petal.

BLEACH

I use bleach sparingly, but I will admit it produces some really beautiful effects. It can be applied with a paintbrush to specific areas of a flower or, for an ombré effect, you can dip the end of a roll of paper in ⅛" of bleach in a glass bowl and set the bleached end down on a protected surface to dry. Bleach bleeds quickly, and much more than you would expect, so use it sparingly, undershooting where you need it. Always work in a well-ventilated area when using bleach. I do not use bleach on flowers that will be worn near my face, as a matter of safety.

COFFEE AND TEA

CHALK

INK AND WATERCOLOR

BLEACH

STAINING PAPER WITH PAPER

BARK PAPER

PAPER-ON-PAPER STAINING

PAPER RESIDUE

STAINING PAPER WITH PAPER

The upside of most crepe paper colors not being water resistant is that they give off their beautiful dyes when wet. This allows you to make a whole rainbow of stains, simply by soaking pieces of crepe in warm water. It can be done in small amounts, with just a few square inches of crepe paper in a few tablespoons of water, or in larger amounts when needed. Most often, I use a stain of equal parts maroon and dark brown crepe paper together. Some of the tutorials prescribe how much water and paper to use, but experiment with your own recipes. Apply stain with a brush, or dip the end of a whole roll in the stain, then unroll on a protected surface and let dry. Dry and save the paper used to make the stain to use as well, as it will have an interesting appearance.

PAPER-ON-PAPER STAINING

Paper-on-paper staining is what I call wetting a strip of darker crepe, placing it on a lighter piece of crepe, and rolling over it with a rolling pin or pressing down with the back of a spoon to transfer the color. This gives a less-solid look than painting the stain on since it won't fill in all the nooks and crannies of the crepe. If using a wooden rolling pin, place a layer of waxed paper between the pin and the wet paper before rolling.

Sometimes the paper you want to extract color from is more water resistant. If you find this is the case, use the "squeeze and soak" method. Wet the paper you are pulling the color from, and squeeze it very tightly over the paper you are trying to stain. There will be a lot of water, but if you try to blot it right away you will remove most of the dye, so it is best to let it soak. Do *not* hang to dry. After a few hours, the color will have sunken in enough that you can pat away most of the water, but allow more time for the paper to dry fully.

BARK PAPER

I love my bark paper, which was an accidental invention. It is a perfect fit for bark, dried leaves, and pods. I discovered this wonderful technique by literally giving a roll of 180 gram #567 light brown and a roll of 180 gram #602 black crepe paper a bath, unfurled in about 8" of water in our bathtub. I reserved most of the murky water that was created to stain paper at a later date, wrung the two rolls out by squeezing them together, and hung them from a tree in our yard for several hours on a sunny day. I was delighted to discover that both rolls had turned into something resembling bark, with swirls of black and gray and occasional flecks of red and warm brown. Two full rolls of crepe are not necessary, just equal amounts of both colors. Squeeze them together underwater, and then again as you wring them out for best effects. Try using dark brown crepe, or substituting deep green or dark blue for the black crepe to create other unique hues.

PAPER RESIDUE

Besides using chalk, another clever way to give the appearance of fallen pollen is to use paper residue. Apply a very thin layer of tacky glue with a paintbrush to the area of the petal where you want the pollen, overlay an outstretched piece of the pollen-colored paper, rub lightly, and peel away immediately. This works best when the color of the pollen is darker than the paper it is being applied to, as demonstrated with the Coral Reef (Oriental) Poppies on page 105.

MY FAVORITE ROSES

After spending the past few years researching and hoarding images of every rose imaginable, I could easily fill an entire book with only paper roses. For now, here are tutorials for my five favorites, from a simple hybrid tea rose to a few fancy David Austin varieties. One is even made in and around an eggshell, for the form and the fun of it.

Most roses have very similar petals with which you can make very different blooms. With some keen observation and the skills you will find on the following pages, you should be able to adapt these templates and directions for any rose in your garden, perhaps with some additional rose dissection on your part. Simply tracing rose petals is sometimes all that is required when creating templates, but remember, by forming and stretching your crepe paper after cutting, the petal you create will always be bigger than the template, so be sure to adjust accordingly. When making paper roses, the most important thing for me is to forget about roses. If you become caught up in your memory of a rose, you may miss out on that magic of letting the little imperfections happen that can make your work truly special.

For details on rose leaves, stems, buds, and more, see pages 188 and 195.

hybrid tea rose

Anything goes when it comes to a hybrid tea rose—there are cultivars in almost every color under the sun. Of its many forms, my favorite possesses a vase-shaped center that loosens up quickly, with relatively few petals. These roses grow on long, single stems, which look nice with just a few leaves and a bud here or there, and make for sweet headpiece fillers.

When using the two-colored doublette crepe paper specified, be mindful of what color is visible to keep your petals consistent throughout. Specific locations for each petal are given, but you can adjust locations or add additional petals if you'd like. If the petals become too square from grooming, simply round them with scissors before attaching to the flower.

The yellow/peach doublette used here can be substituted with yellow/light salmon doublette for a subtle variation. Brushing any doublette crepe color with strong black coffee will bring the paper colors together to create very natural-looking rose petals. Coffee used on pale pink/apricot doublette will yield a café au lait hue very close to the hybrid Julia's Rose. Or try making a Neil Diamond, whose candy-striped pattern (Pattern 4) can be found on page 114.

Heavier papers can also be used for more durability, but, due to their stretch, the petals will be larger and somewhat distorted and will need to be trimmed down to the proper size and shape after grooming.

Tacky glue

Yellow/peach (or any bicolored) doublette crepe paper

180 gram #562 dusty green crepe paper

Blending paintbrush

Mod Podge

Deep-pink or mauve chalk

Light-green floral tape

16-gauge green cloth-covered stem wire

Leaves (see page 195) and buds (see page 188)

1 Bend the top of the stem wire down 1¼" and up ¾", creating a tight, S-shaped curve. Wrap floral tape around tightly into a ½"-wide by ¾"-tall bud with ¼" of wire at the top. Cut three HR1, three HR2, and twelve HR3 petals from yellow/peach doublette. Rub the top quarter of the peach side of all petals with deep-pink chalk, then blend with a paintbrush. Cup the yellow side of the three HR1 petals, then lightly stretch and bend the top edges back over a hat pin.

2 Cover the bud and wire with doublette. Attach the three HR1 petals, yellow side in, with light tacky glue on their cupped bellies. Set the first petal just above the wire, the second across from the first, and the third staggered from the second ⅛", each a hair higher than the last.

The remaining petals should face peach side up or in. Give each a small, rounded V-shaped cut in the middle of the top edges, cutting a slightly deeper and less rounded V in each step. Stretch the petals lightly at both sides of the V.

Cup the three HR2 petals and bend the tips backward using your fingernails to avoid a curl. Attach the first with glue at the belly, staggered from the HR1 petals, the tip up 1/16" from the center. Attach the second petal across from the first, tucking one edge underneath the first, then add the third, staggered ⅛" from the second, each rising 1/16" higher than the last.

3 Carefully trim away the loose petal bottoms and smooth the cut edges underneath the bud with glue.

Cup three HR3 petals deeply. Roll the top edges back lightly, angling 30 to 40 degrees downward. Attach the first with glue at the belly anyplace it will sit naturally, and call that position 4:30. Following the petal layouts in the photos like a clock face, place the second petal at 10:30, and the third at 4:30 again, with its left edge loose.

Set all at the same height, a little more than 1/16" up from the previous petals.

4 Cup an additional two HR3 petals, rolling the petal sides back, then angle the top edges downward. Attach with glue at the bottom ½", placing one at 12 o'clock with the tip slightly above the inner petals. Gather the very bottom of the second petal and place it at 7:30, tucked under the loose petal from step 3, falling open but aligned at the top with the inner petals.

5 Next, roll two HR3 petals backward halfway down their faces, then stretch the backsides to make them convex. Cup the bottom third of the faces to be concave, gather the very bottoms, and roll the sides back a little. Attach one at 1:30. Lightly crumple then smooth the top half of the other, allowing it to bend back more and look slightly weathered. Reroll the sides and end backward and attach at 7 o'clock, falling open.

6 Repeat step 5 for the remaining five petals, gathering the bases minimally, and rolling the top edges back tightly at dramatic angles that meet at the top. Crush and smooth one or two petals to allow them to bend back near their midpoints. Attach at 2 and 4, then 12 and 9:30, and 7 o'clock, some sitting almost flat.

7 Fold an outstretched piece of 1⅞"-tall by 2"-long 180 gram #562 dusty green crepe into five layers and cut per the CLX1 guide. Cup each sepal and tint the convex side with Mod Podge mixed with pink chalk dust. Glue the calyx to the bottom of the petals tightly around the stem, evenly spaced, with the tinted side up, then carefully curve the sepals to point down, then back up at the tips.

8 Wrap the stem in floral tape, adding single or multiple leaf sets and buds as desired.

iceberg floribunda rose

Tacky glue

100 gram yellow orange
crepe paper

180 gram #575
bright yellow crepe paper

White doublette
crepe paper

180 gram #567
light brown crepe paper
(optional)

180 gram moss green
crepe paper

Lemon-yellow chalk

Blending paintbrush

20-gauge green
cloth-covered stem wire

Leaves (see page 195) and
buds (see page 188)

Throughout this book, it will become clear that I am a sucker for a white flower with a yellow center, like the Iceberg Floribunda, which is a sweet little white-and-yellow gem. This tutorial uses a trick I came up with to make realistic stamens, and it's one that you can parlay into all sorts of paper flower making. These densely clustered and abundant roses are lovely on their own, but I think you should consider making a copious amount of them to get the full floribunda effect.

As with other tutorials in this book, the petal placements given are my best suggestions to keep your rose from looking like another flower. It is important to avoid placing one petal right behind another in this case, because this particular rose can look like a camellia if you're not careful.

When cutting the petals for this rose, it is best to cut them one at a time with a folded or half template aligned with a fold in the paper to keep the petals symmetrical and uniform in size before styling them. The width of the petal where it meets the stem must be small in order to prevent the petal base from wrapping around the flower, closing it up. Make sure you cut the petal bases as slender as shown on the template for proper gathering and attachment.

1 For the stamen, start with a 1¼"-tall by 3½"-long piece of outstretched 100 gram yellow orange crepe. Apply tacky glue along the top ¼" of the strip, then roll and fold the very top edge down onto itself three or four times, reapplying glue as needed to adhere, creating a ¹⁄₁₆" rim. Laminate a piece of outstretched 180 gram #575 bright yellow crepe paper to each side of the strip just below the rim. Cut the piece down to ¾" tall, then finely fringe the rolled edge with the inner part of your scissors. Let dry for a half hour.

Glue outstretched bright yellow crepe over the top ½" of the stem wire and hook it down ¼". When the stamen fringe is dry, cut a piece 1⅛" long, reserving the rest for other roses. Gather it onto itself and roll tightly back and forth several times just below the rim between your thumb and forefinger. Apply glue to the bottom of the strip, interlock with the hook, and wrap around, with the top of the hook set halfway down into the fringe.

2 Cut two IFR1 and three IFR2 petals from white doublette. Gently cup the top quarter of the IFR1 and IFR2 petals at their backsides so they are convex and bending backward a bit at the top edges. Cup the bottom third of the front of each petal, then finish by holding the top center of each one and pushing one side forward while pulling the other side back, creating a small crease in the top edges. Vary the treatments so not all the petals look the same. One IFR1 petal should be more cupped, while the other should be slightly broader. The bottom ⅜" of the broader one should be gathered with glue so the petal is longer, while the bottom ⅝" of the more cupped one should be gathered for a shorter petal. The three IFR2 petals should be cupped and groomed similarly, each gathered ⅝" at the base. Ripple each IFR2 a little along one or both sides of the top edge, reinforcing the convex tops and

concave bellies after rippling. Round any top corners that have become overly square in the process. Rub lemon-yellow chalk into the bottom ¼" of each petal.

Bend each petal back at its base and attach to the flower at the center just below the fringe, angled about 45 degrees upward. Remember where 12 o'clock is on your flower if you would like to follow the petal layouts in the photographs. Place the smaller IFR1 petal at 2 o'clock with the larger staggered behind it at the 1:30 position. Place the three IFR2 petals at 2:30, 4:30, and 10:30. Bend the stamen tips against a hat pin or skewer, then tousle the stamen fringe so it looks loose and multidirectional.

3 Cut six IFR3 petals from white doublette. Ripple each side of the top edge lightly, cup the backside gently halfway down the petal, then cup the face two-thirds of the way back up. Deeply crease and divot at the center of the top edge, reinforcing the slight convex bent back top edge if needed afterward. Trim to maintain the slightly rounded tip and curve any square edges if overstretched. Rub yellow chalk into petals that will appear right below the stamens. Bend each back at the base and glue at the 3 and then 7:30, 6:30, 9, 10:30, and 12 o'clock positions. You may find some petals sit better in some spots than others, so test them before gluing. Try slipping the edges in to overlap IFR2 petals occasionally to help them sit more naturally around the flower.

4 Cut thirteen IFR4 petals from white doublette. Groom similarly to the IFR3 petals, but make the warps, ripples, bends, and divots slightly more obvious. Bend each back at the base and glue the first six at 12:30 and 5:30, then 4:30 and 8:30, then 7:30 and 11:30.

CONTINUED

1

2

3

4

5

6

7

8

5 Attach the final seven IFR4 petals at 12, 1:30, 3:30, 7, 10, 10:30, and 9 o'clock, angling slightly downward. Adjust the petal locations to fill in around the flower, and slip the edges in to overlap other petals if needed for a more natural fit. If the rose looks at all unfinished to you, feel free to add a few more filler petals here and there. Squeeze the entire flower base to compact and taper as much as possible, cutting away any petal bases that make it look too jagged or uneven.

6 Since this rose grows in clusters, it is nice to add some variety if making a number of them. For a rose a little past its prime, replace the yellow stamens with a similarly rolled single strip of outstretched 180 gram #567 light brown crepe. Split the top edges of a few of the petals, setting the smaller inner petals more inward and upward while curving the edges of the larger petals back more dramatically.

7 For the calyx, fold an outstretched piece of 1⅞"-tall by 2"-long 180 gram moss green crepe into five layers and cut per the CLX1 guide, then spindle the paper before opening it up. Cup the wider portion at the bottom of each sepal. Apply tacky glue along the uncut bottom edge and ⅛" up each sepal on the cupped side, then attach the calyx at the intersection of the flower base and the underside of the petals. Taking care not to pull the calyx back off of the flower, groom each sepal to hang back down, with the tips swooping back upward a tad. Wrap the base and stem of each flower with outstretched moss green crepe.

To create a flowering branch, attach three rose stems together in a trident formation, wrapping together with moss green crepe. Attach a leaf stem a few inches down from that intersection, adding another rose across from the leaf stem if desired. Olive green doublette rose leaves with a stem of light-green floral tape wiped with crimson liquid concentrated watercolor will complement the moss green rose stems nicely, but the leaves can also match the calyx for a brighter appearance overall.

8 These roses are often competing for space at the end of their branches, so arrange them in crowded clusters reaching for the sun. Single rose stems come off the main branch horizontally with a swoop upward at the end, as do rosebuds. Single, smaller leaves can be placed at intersections of two or more rose stems, which can help to cover awkward or bulky intersections.

english roses two ways

Tacky glue

Hot glue

180 gram #600/4
rose ombré crepe paper

Green crepe paper of
your choice for optional
calyces and stem wrap

16-gauge green cloth-
covered stem wire

Light-green floral tape

Paper-covered plastic
egg, papier-mâché egg,
or jumbo empty, rinsed
chicken's egg (Rose I
only; see Note)

Leaves (see page 195)

Brown floral tape
(optional)

Being neither a botanist nor a rose specialist, the exact names of the English roses I like to make elude me. The difference between famed rose breeder David Austin's A Shropshire Lad and William Morris roses might come down to just a fold, or a hue, or the ripple on the edge of a petal. So instead, I give you English Rose I and English Rose II, two different forms to use as a base for many other English roses by just tweaking the color or petal treatment. English Rose I is cleverly built in and around a plastic egg, or an empty chicken's eggshell if you dare. This works beautifully and was partially informed by how I build my large-scale pieces.

When working with ombré paper here, the lighter hue should be oriented toward the top of the petals. Swiping your fingers or petal bases through glue can make quicker work of these roses, and I recommend completing one row of petals before moving down to the next to avoid confusion. Usually I am specific about how many rows of petals there should be, but here it really depends on how the flower looks as you go along. Follow the petal layouts and instructions the best you can, but add or omit petals and rows whenever it feels right.

Note: To prepare the paper-covered plastic egg or papier-mâché egg used for English Rose I, use scissors to make a ⅛" hole in the bottom end and remove the top ¾" to ⅞" of the tapered end just before the egg tapers inward. For chicken eggs, use a series of gentle pin pricks with a thumbtack to cut the top ¾" to ⅞" of the shell away and create a ⅛" hole in the bottom. Discard the egg white and yolk, then rinse and dry the shell before using.

ENGLISH ROSE I

1 Cut 90 ER1 petals from an outstretched section of rose ombré crepe paper located between 3¼" and 5⅛" from the end of the roll. Create a crease up the center to the tips of 60 pink faces and 30 white (uncolored) faces of the petals with your thumbnail. Set 20 of the latter petals aside for use in step 4.

2 Use 60 pink-faced and 10 white-faced petals to create a random assortment of cupped stacks of two or three petals, with either pink or white faces up, as well as 10 single petals. These will all be clustered together to form the rose's center. Crimp the petal bases of each stack together with tacky glue, then lightly roll and crumple the sides of half the stacks over a hat pin, re-creasing the centers afterward to smooth the petals. Fold five single petals and seven stacks onto themselves lengthwise, then tacky glue the other five single petals to the sides of five random stacks, cupping them. Gather any five stacks together with tacky glue, the petals sitting as vertically as possible, nesting some stacks in others, some turned to the side, and some to the center. Place strategically so the rose's center appears more pink than white. Make a tiny hook at the top of the stem wire and hot glue the side of the petal cluster's base to it.

3 Interlock the remaining stacks and single petals similarly. Once the cluster is nickel-size, even if lopsided, position the petal tips ¼" higher, then another ¼" higher as you near the outer edge. Face any folded stacks inward or to the side, and slide the folded single petals in to fill gaps. Fill out and round the outer perimeter with inward facing stacks, bringing the diameter to 2". Squeeze the base together and wrap at the stem with pink crepe to secure.

4 Cover the cut rim of the egg in pink crepe. Pull the stem wire through the bottom hole in the egg until the petal tips are ⅝" above the rim, making the full flower height around 2¼". Secure with floral tape wrapped around the wire just below the egg, tacky gluing the tape end 1" up the side of the egg. Tacky glue the white inside faces of the reserved 20 ER1 petals snugly around the rim with tips aligned, obscuring the white backsides of the inner petals. Place a second row down ¹⁄₁₆", staggered one-third of the way from the first row of petals.

5 Cut 20 type ER2 petals from outstretched ombré crepe located between 5" and 7" from the end of the roll. Crease up the white sides, then curl the top edges lightly back over a hat pin. Attach snugly to the flower with tacky glue halfway up their white insides in two rows, stepping each row down ¹⁄₁₆". Stagger the petals in relation to the petals above, creating a jagged diagonal slope down from row to row with the slanted top edges of the petals. Follow this loosely, avoiding any petal layouts that appear too regular.

Note: For the ER3 to 5 petals in steps 6 to 8, stretch the paper in between your hands to flatten, but don't force it to be completely outstretched.

6 Cut 28 type ER3 petals from ombré crepe located between 7" and 9" from the end of the roll. Cup with the pink side away from you and curl the angled top edges lightly back over a hat pin. Stagger and attach in two rows per step 5, stepping the first row down ¹⁄₁₆" from ER2 petals above, and the next row down ¹⁄₈".

7 Cut 20 type ER4 petals from ombré crepe located between 7" and 9" from the end of the roll. Cup, curl, stagger, and attach the petals in two rows as in step 6, stepping down ¹⁄₈" with each row, locating the petal tips approximately midway down the flower.

8 Cut 8 to 12 type ER5 petals from the lightest ombré crepe at the center of the roll. Cup each petal and stretch the bases to widen. Cup the backsides on either side of the V, then ripple the top edges with your thumbnail, or roll them back or crush some over a hat pin. Attach two or three rows, with tacky glue one-third up the inside of the petals, taking care not to overlap them. The first row should fall slightly open with the tips near the height of the petals above. The bottom rows should cup the flower's base then fall open, the petals placed equally in between the petals above. See the previous rose tutorials and page 188 for calyces and rose stem details.

ENGLISH ROSE II

1 Cut 24 ER6 petals from the section of rose ombré crepe paper located between 2¾" and 5" from the end of the roll. Reserve two petals and arrange the rest into six stacks of three and two stacks of two, pink faces up, staggering petals down ¹⁄₁₆" from back to front. Adhere the petal stacks together with ½" tacky glue at their bases. Cup each stack and single petal, fold onto themselves, and pinch the bases together with ⅝" tacky glue up the inside. Crush both sides of each stack and single petal back over a hat pin.

2 Reopen and smooth the stacks by running the width of your thumbnail lightly up their centers. Bend the bases of the stacks and single petals back 45 degrees at a point ⅝" from their bottoms. Hold each stack closed and trim a portion of the petal edges and tops off, using ER10 as a guide, giving them somewhat bevel-cut faces. Style some folded tight, some with faces fully open, and some in between.

3 Make a tiny hook at the top of the stem wire and tacky glue the bottoms of the bent bases to the top ½" of the wire, squeezing together frequently. Attach the two folded single petals closer to the center, sitting slightly lower. Face some stacks straight upward and others nested or turned to the side. Hold together a minute or two when done while the glue sets.

4 Carefully snip away extra paper at the petal bases without disconnecting the flower from the stem. Tacky glue floral tape to the base and wrap tightly to the stem when set to secure. Cut 24 ER7 petals from ombré crepe located between 4⅞" and 7" from the end of the roll. Cup their pink sides, cut a sharp ⅛"-deep V in the top edges, and curl the edges back lightly over a hat pin. Focusing on the face of the flower as you go, apply tacky glue to the bottom ⅝" of each petal and press to the undersides of the petals above. The tips of the innermost ER7 petals should align with the height of the outer ER6 petal tips. Nest stacks of inner petals inside two overlapping ER7 petals, and slide other ER7 petals between the inner petals so they tilt partially sideways. Fold some onto themselves alone or nested, and wedge them in between other petals to fill in. Whenever possible, pinch the bases of the outer petals around the undersides of the inner petal stacks to secure. If large gaps form between petal layers, press closer together with dabs of tacky glue.

5 Continue with the ER7 petals, rounding and filling the flower to around 3½" in diameter.

6 Cut 12 to 14 ER8 petals from ombré crepe located between 6¾" and 9" from the end of the roll. Cup their pink centers and cut a sharp ⅛"-deep V in the center of the top edges. Stretch the petal edges, then curl each side back over a hat pin. Attach in two rows to the undersides of the petals above per step 5, using hot glue if the base is too wet with tacky glue. The upper row of ER8 petals should extend approximately ¼" out from the petals above them, positioned to cup several smaller petals above when possible. Stagger the second row in no particular pattern until it looks even, extending out a hair beyond the first, with the diameter around 4⅛".

7 Cut 24 ER9 petals from the lightest ombré crepe at the center of the roll. Cup the centers and stretch the top edges to widen before cutting a sharp ¼" V in the center. Curl the sides back over a skewer, then stretch the bases to give the petals some floppiness. Bend the petals back ⅛" at their bases and attach snugly to the bottom of the flower in three or four rows with hot glue applied to the face above the bend. The first two rows should cup upward and hold closer to the petals above. The bottom rows can flop out and downward, or you can keep them cupped upward if you like. The petals should be applied in a loose stagger from row to row, each one extending out between 1/16" and ⅛" from the row above. Trim away unglued bent petal bases.

8 If a calyx is desired, use guide CLX1 in a green crepe paper of your choice and cut and attach per the previous rose tutorials or the calyx instruction on page 188, which includes more rose stem details. Try attaching leaves with brown floral tape for an interesting stem.

my very favorite rose

(OR, A VERY LARGE ROSA PERLE D'OR)

Tacky glue

Pale pink/apricot doublette crepe paper

Light salmon/light rose doublette crepe paper

Orange/red orange doublette crepe paper

180 gram #600/1 raspberry ombré crepe paper

Orange single-ply thin crepe paper fold

180 gram #568 dark brown crepe paper

Crimson liquid watercolor

Wide, firm paintbrush

16-gauge green cloth-wrapped stem wire

Leaves (see page 195)

Resembling a Perle d'Or rose that grew a little too big and turned a little too orange, this flower is an amalgam of my favorite rose forms and colors. It is based on a stunning photograph I saw a few years ago of a climbing rose, which I immediately made out of paper and revisited for this book.

This is hands-down one of the fussiest flowers I've included here, and you might think I've lost my mind when you read it for the first time. But I have made a sincere effort to capture the wild center of this rose and to give it a lot of movement and depth of color. As involved as this tutorial is, it gets much easier once you are out of the center, and it will most definitely take your breath away when you are finished. And your second one will go much quicker.

The laminated paper in the tutorial should be used soon after it is glued together or it will become too stiff to manipulate, but wait five minutes or so to cut the petals after laminating or it will be too wet. The orange side of the laminated petals should always face out on the flower. Squeeze the base together frequently to keep it tidy. This rose is so beautiful that I don't bother with a calyx, but you can add one if you'd like.

1 Bend the top ¼" of the stem wire down. Cut 10 PDOR1 petals from pale pink/apricot doublette and cover the end of the wire with a scrap. Cup all 10 petals, two pale side out, the rest pale side in. Gather the bottoms with tacky glue. Nest the two pale-side-out petals together and tacky glue the concave face of the pair ¹⁄₁₆" above the covered wire. Run your thumbnail from the gathered base to the tip of the next petal, creating a deep crease. Attach 1" above the wire, opposite the nested pair. Create two more nested pairs, crushing the sides along a hat pin, then creasing up the centers with your thumbnail. Glue the back of one nested pair directly across from the first pair, tops aligned, then glue the other pair sideways inside the previous one, the top halfway between the highest and lowest petals. Crush, then crease the centers of two more petals and attach them side by side, folded and facing inward, ¼" lower and just behind and outward from the tallest petal. Attach the last petal opposite the previous pair, ¼" above the top of the wire.

2 Cut three PDOR2 petals from pale pink/apricot doublette, one from light salmon/light rose doublette, one from orange/red orange doublette, and one from outstretched 180 gram #600/1 raspberry ombré crepe paper, 6" from the end of the roll. Orient your rose with the tallest petal from step 1 at the 6 o'clock position. Cup the three pale pink petals with the darker side in, crush the edges along a hat pin, and crease each up the center. Using tacky glue to gather and attach petals as you go, nest two together at 8 o'clock, folded faces inward and tips aligned with the tallest petal. Position the single creased petal at 9 o'clock, ¼" lower than the previous pair. Cup, crush, and crease up the center of the one salmon/rose petal, rose side out. Fold closed and slide into the center of the flower at 10:30, the tip aligned with the tallest petal. Cup the remaining two petals darker sides

out, and center a small V-shaped cut in the top edge of each. Curl and crush the top ¼" of the orange petal backward over your hat pin, then smooth out with your fingers. Place at 2 o'clock, down ⅜" from the tallest petals. Curl the edge of the raspberry petal back on either side of the V at an angle, then attach at 3 o'clock, ⅛" down from the orange petal.

3 Cut six PDOR1 petals from light salmon/light rose doublette and three from pale pink/apricot doublette. Cup three of the salmon/rose petals with the rose side out and gather the bottom half of each. Continuing to tacky glue as you go, nest two petals together at 7 o'clock, just above the lowest petals. Add the other at 4 o'clock, ¹⁄₁₆" higher than the previous petals. Cup, crush, and crease another salmon/rose petal and slide into the center at 8 o'clock, ⅜" down from the tallest petals. Cut off and cup the top ⅜" of the last two salmon/rose petals, rose side out, and gather the bottoms together. Place into the center of the flower facing outward at 1:30. Cup the three pale pink/apricot petals with the pale side in. Cut a V in the top of one, curl down the top ⅛", and place ½" down from the tallest petals at 6 o'clock. Cut another in half, cup the top and gather its bottom, and place folded and facing inward at 10:30, ⅛" above the tiny petal pair in the center. Cup, crush, and crease the last petal. Place at 1 o'clock, just inside the orange petal with the adjacent pale petals.

4 Cut three PDOR1 petals from outstretched raspberry crepe, 6" from the end of the roll. Gently curve the raspberry face of two petals inward, gather the bases, and attach slightly staggered at 11 o'clock, tops down ¼" from the tallest petals. Cup the raspberry face of the final petal, gather at the base, fold inward, and place around 9 o'clock, down ⅜" from adjacent petals.

CONTINUED

5 Rip 2"-tall strips of orange single-ply crepe paper against the grain and use a wide, firm paintbrush to laminate them with a light layer of tacky glue to the apricot side of pale pink/apricot doublette. Match the direction of the paper grain on both papers. Apply glue to the doublette in a slightly taller swath than the height of the orange paper to assure the orange paper completely adheres. Position the orange strips with minimum ½" of apricot paper above each one.

Cut five PDOR3 petals with their full height in orange, and nine PDOR4, 15 PDOR5, and 12 PDOR6 petals with the petal tips ¼" to ⅜" into the apricot and the rest of the petal orange.

6 In general, the petals in steps 6 to 8 should splay out ¼" to ⅜" from the ones in the previous step, and should very gradually sit lower on the flower as you go. Cup the lighter side of five orange PDOR3 petals and curl the top edges back and down at slight angles. Nest and stagger four of them down and over about ¹⁄₁₆", as shown. Glue together and attach the highest of the four at 6 o'clock, ½" down from the top of the tallest center petals, the rest spanning counterclockwise. Add the fifth PDOR3 petal at 7 o'clock, ⅜" down from the previous set. Cup five PDOR4 petals and curl and swoop them backward by pulling the back of the top third of each along your hat pin, with your thumb at the face. Gather at their bases and add a crease by running a fingernail all the way up the backside of each. Attach two staggered at 8 o'clock, tops aligned with the orange petal at 6 o'clock. Attach two more staggered at 1 o'clock, the bend of the swoop of the petals aligned with the adjacent orange petal. Cup six PDOR5 petals, gather their bases, swoop their tops backward, and curl the top edges back a bit as well. Place a single one at 3 o'clock, its top aligned with the raspberry petal it cups. Stagger two with centered creases up their backsides at

4:30, ⅛" lower than the previous pair. Place the last three at 9:30, 10, and 9 o'clock, in that order, sitting slightly upright at the same height as the previous petals. Place the fifth PDOR4 from earlier in this step at 3:30, ¹⁄₁₆" lower than the petals it hugs.

7 The petals in this step should begin to even out the flower's perimeter a bit. Cup all 12 PDOR6 petals, then stretch the backside of the top of each petal to be slightly wider and convex at the face. Pull a deep crease up the back of each petal, and curl the top edges at either side of the center V back deeply. Attach one to the flower at 7 o'clock with ½" of its face visible. Set the remaining 11 petals aside for use in step 8. Cup four PDOR4 petals and give a deep crease up their backs. Roll the top edges back ¼", giving each a little crumple and then smoothing it out. Place two at 11:30, the outer one turned a bit to give an irregular look. Stagger the other two near 9 o'clock. Cup the remaining nine PDOR5 petals, gather the bases, stretch the back of the tops, crease up the backsides, and deeply swoop each. Place them at 12, 2, 4, 6, 8, and 10 o'clock, then at 3:30, 4:30, and 6:30.

8 Place the remaining PDOR6 petals from step 7 around the rose, staggering with the other petals but avoiding an overly regular pattern. Glue ¾" up the face of each to be sure they aren't opening too low on the flower. The petals should swoop down to almost obscure the base and extend out past the step 7 petals around ⅜", resulting in a flower face approximately 4" in diameter. Wrap the stem with outstretched dark brown crepe paper and paint with crimson watercolor for a lovely reddish brown stem. If adding leaves, wrap their stems with crepe to match the main rose stem.

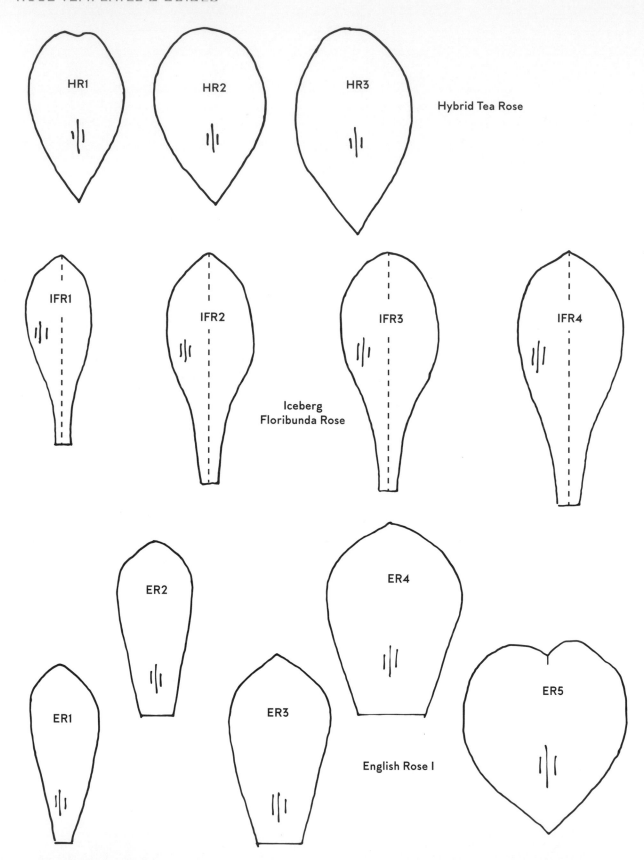

HR1

HR2

HR3

Hybrid Tea Rose

IFR1

IFR2

IFR3

IFR4

Iceberg
Floribunda Rose

ER2

ER4

ER1

ER3

ER5

English Rose I

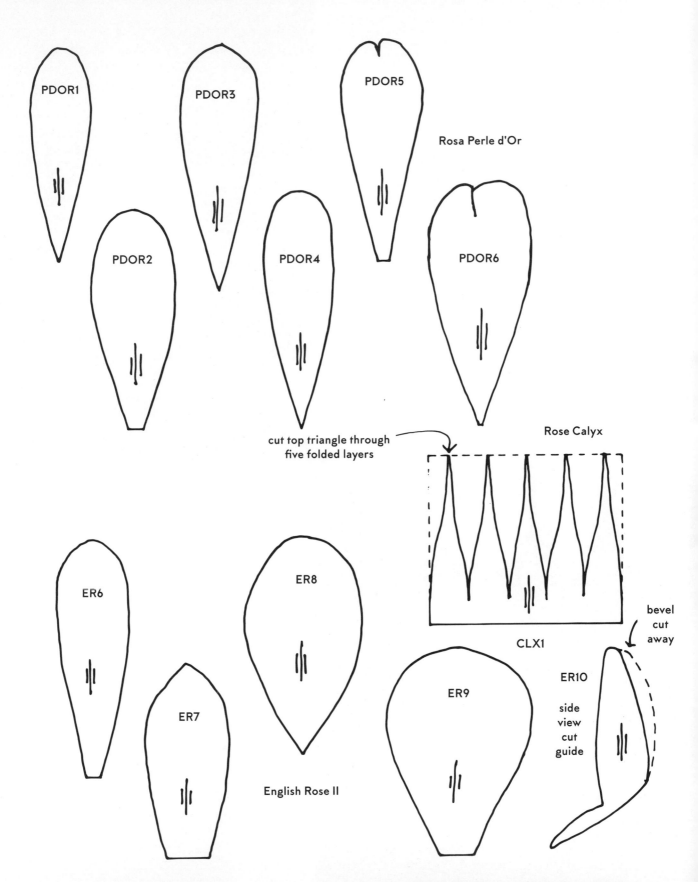

PDOR1

PDOR3

PDOR5

Rosa Perle d'Or

PDOR2

PDOR4

PDOR6

cut top triangle through
five folded layers

Rose Calyx

CLX1

ER6

ER8

bevel
cut
away

ER7

ER9

ER10

side
view
cut
guide

English Rose II

playing with color

I am a stickler when it comes to realism in form. Color, however, is another thing altogether. Crepe paper comes in so many luscious hues, it's hard to work with just the colors that occur in the natural world. I can happily forget about realism when it comes to color. I like to wear a spooky crown of black paper roses and carnations or make a bouquet undeniably bridal by filling it with bright white versions of the bride's favorite otherwise colorful flowers. Working in monotone can be very interesting and create beautiful effects, especially if you use one color from the top of the flower to the tip of the stem. When I teach paper flower workshops, I sometimes bring a basket full of crepe paper in a wide range of colors for my students to use. It expands my own palette when I see the colors my pupils choose to make their flowers. There is always someone making something in a color I never would have considered, opening my eyes a little more to how others see the world. It's one of the best parts of teaching.

Using ombré paper is a fun way to play with color. You can use the rose and candy corn ombrés to capture the natural fading and gradual color shifts within a single blossom or throughout an entire bush. On top of that, you can find ombré paper in shades like sky blue–to–white–to–sky blue and bright green–to–lemon yellow–to–bright green. Use that nuanced paper to really turn your flowers and leaves on their heads.

At the end of the day, as much as I love to study and replicate flowers in the most realistic ways possible, paper flower making is an art form, which means allowing for personal expression as much through the choices we make as the skills we possess. So, yes, even though I am a stickler, please, make your violets red and your roses blue. I won't stop you.

FRINGE-CENTERED FLOWERS

In reality, most every flower has some sort of fringe-like element to it, either at the center cluster of stamens or occasionally at the edge of certain petals. There are lots of these little bits lying in wait inside of roses and dahlias and such, even if you can't see them. The fringe-centered flowers included here are the ones that give a full, overt presentation of their center parts. There are dozens more I could have included, but these four selections have techniques and templates that can be parlayed into a host of other flowers, like daisies and asters and black-eyed Susans, many of which are in the same families. Quite a few of the flowers in the remainder of chapter 2 build on these "fringe elements" as well.

FINE FRINGE

ROLLED AND TWISTED FRINGE

LAMINATED FRINGE

COMPOSITE FRINGE CENTERS

fringe types & techniques

These are the types of fringe used in the book, and my advice on how to make the best fringe possible. In general, the finer the fringe, the finer the flower. Even though I am a stickler for detail, simple fringe can be used for the center of any flower and still look lovely.

FINE FRINGE

With very few exceptions, the fringe used in this book is called "fine fringe," meaning it is cut as finely as possible. To create fine fringe, hold the strip of paper you are fringing between the thumb and forefinger of your non-cutting hand. Set the bottom blade of your scissors down across the other three fingers on that same hand. Keep your scissors set in that one spot while you feed the paper through the tips of the scissors like a sewing machine with your thumb and forefinger. Cut rapidly, moving just the top blade up and down. Adjust the speed at which you slide the paper through the scissor blades, coordinating with the speed of your cutting movements until your cutting is both fast and fine. Pieces of the fringe will go flying in the process, but there are usually so many little filaments that it won't make a difference.

LAMINATED FRINGE

I created laminated fringes in order to be able to stagger the colors on some stamens to depict the top anthers and the longer filaments that hold them. In some cases, the fine fringing technique described previously works perfectly on laminated paper, but if the paper becomes either too hard or too damp with glue, it is best to use the place where your two scissor blades meet, aka the crotch, to do the cutting. Always let the glue set up about 5 minutes or as directed before attempting to fringe a laminated strip to avoid it turning to pulp on your scissor blades.

ROLLED AND TWISTED FRINGE

These fringes are used for larger elements in flower centers here and elsewhere in the book. Wider fringe pieces are brushed lightly with tacky glue four or five at a time, then rolled onto themselves between your thumb and forefinger along their centerlines until they are rounded and smooth. Sometimes they are pointed, and sometimes the tips are folded down while being rolled to create a bulbous end. Usually it is easier to twist wide laminated fringe than to roll it, with the thickness of the laminated paper and the moisture of the glue being factors.

COMPOSITE FRINGE CENTERS

Composite fringe centers are realistic-looking flower centers that contain two or more types of fringe. Examples are open dahlia and chocolate cosmos centers, which each have fine fringe surrounded by rolled or twisted fringe.

FRINGING TIPS

- For fringing, find scissors that work easily for you. I find that the thinner 4"-long blades found on simple kitchen scissors work best for me.

- Always cut fringe deeply enough to leave only ⅛" of the paper strip uncut at the bottom, unless otherwise noted.

- When wrapping fringe around a stem wire, do not stretch while wrapping unless instructed to do so. This can vary throughout a tutorial, or even in a single step of the tutorial. If the fringe rips while wrapping, just reattach it with glue.

- Some flowers call for the fringe to be spindled after cutting for best results.

california tree poppy

Tacky glue

Hot glue

60 gram #296 yellow crepe paper

100 gram white crepe paper

Sharp graphite pencil

16-gauge green cloth-covered stem wire

Leaves (see page 195)

This simple, gorgeous flower is whimsically known as the "fried-egg flower" due to its appearance. It is native to southern California and northern Mexico, growing on large shrubs, as opposed to individual stems from the ground like other types of poppies. I love to sculpt the simple, fluffy yellow centers and then surround them with pleated, crumpled petals in all states of unfurling and opening. I often omit the leaves when making an arrangement that includes this poppy. They make such a statement on their own, so curious and tall.

There are two petal sizes included in this tutorial, the smaller representing the size of the flower as it first opens up, the larger for the flower as it expands during its season. Do not mix the two petal sizes on one bloom, but do feel free to make some windblown poppies with just one or two petals. They add a nice touch of realism, or whimsy, depending on how you look at it.

1 Cut eleven ½"-tall by 3"-long strips of 60 gram #296 yellow crepe paper, keeping uniform by drawing light pencil guidelines on the crepe before cutting if needed. Finely fringe each strip. Hook the top of the stem wire a scant ¼". Apply tacky glue to the bottom of one yellow fringe strip, interlock with the hook, and wrap evenly around the top of the wire. Round the base of the fringe with your fingers if lopsided at the hook. Open up the fringe and add a touch of tacky glue deep inside. Groom into a conical shape, then wrap with a small segment of ½"-tall yellow paper, wrapping the top tighter than the base. The fringe should protrude from the top of the cone just a hair.

2 Spindle each of the remaining ten fringe strips and unfurl. One at a time, apply tacky glue and wrap around the base of the cone, being careful not to stretch as you wrap. The top of the first layer of spindled fringe should sit ¹⁄₁₆" above the top of the cone. Each of the following layers should step down a scant ¹⁄₁₆" below the one before it.

3 Using a hat pin, gently brush the yellow layers down and away from the middle to shape a round, fluffy center. Pull the layers away from the base of the center cone, then use the pencil to poke all around where the base meets the fringe to darken that intersection. Use tiny scissors to round the center further if desired. Use the hat pin against your thumb to curl up the ends of the fringe a bit. Go back and forth between curling up and fluffing down for best results.

4 Create two petals at a time by folding two layers of 100 gram white crepe paper along the grain. Align the fold-line edge of template TP-Large or TP-Small along the paper fold, then cut around the template. Repeat another two times to create six petals of the same size for each flower, less if you want it to appear as if petals have fallen away.

To give the petals their pleated, wrinkled look, fold each petal into a tight accordion in the direction of the paper grain and spindle tightly. Gently unfurl each petal without pulling the creases flat. Stretch each petal very lightly across its bottom half and bend lightly with your fingers to create a scooped shape. While petals can be uniform, more often than not the inner three petals will scoop up while the lower three are more horizontal, with drooping edges.

5 Accentuate the crumpled appearance of some petals with random folds across their faces and tiny jagged bumps cut into their tops. Lightly crease some upward along their centerlines and allow the sides to droop down, and roll and mangle others at their ends along a hat pin.

6 Apply ¼" of tacky glue to the bottom of each petal and gather by pinching, taking care not to cup the face of the petal. Bend the pinched end back, then snip it off just below the bend. Add a touch of tacky glue at the sides of the petals near the base, and smooth the sides toward the bottom to taper in a bit. Space the three inner petals equally around the flower, attaching to the underside of the yellow center with hot glue at the bottom ¼" of the face of each petal.

7 Attach the outer three petals similarly, equally spaced, filling the gaps between the inner three petals. Keep the intersection where the petals meet the stem under the flower neat and tidy.

8 Experiment with different crumpled petal forms. The stem does not require wrapping, unless you choose to add leaves.

chocolate cosmos

Tacky glue

Hot glue

180 gram #568
dark brown crepe paper

100 gram yellow orange
crepe paper

100 gram green tea,
limon, or yellow
crepe paper

Olive green doublette
crepe paper (optional)

Red ink or crimson liquid
concentrated watercolor

Water

Wide, soft paintbrush

20-gauge green cloth-
covered stem wire

Leaves (see page 196)

The chocolate cosmos is one of just a few flowers in this book with a single row of petals. It has the most mysterious color, sometimes appearing black; sometimes deep, deep red; sometimes brown. I try to capture a bit of that mystery by embedding brown crepe with red stain before beginning to work with it, applying more layers of color as the flower comes together. The flower will be deep red when finished, but will mellow over time to a reddish brown that is hard to define, which is what we are going for. To avoid red fingertips, wear protective gloves while staining strips and petals.

I like to style the petals with concave centers and convex edges and ends, but they can also simply swoop upward or have ridges like the garden cosmos, so take a look at those pictured on page 100 (step 4) if you want to mix it up.

The center of this flower is composite fringe and a little complex. It looks great, but as with any fringe-centered flower, plain fringe made from the stained paper will work just fine. If the flower head begins to come loose from the stem, add hot glue inside the base. Adding leaves low on the stem where they occur naturally can make it difficult for the flowers to fit properly in a vase and can interrupt their long, tall profile, but add them if you'd like.

1 Prepare a stain using 8 drops of red ink or crimson liquid concentrated watercolor in 2 teaspoons water. Stain three 2"-tall by 5½"-long strips of 180 gram #568 dark brown crepe paper, making 1" streaks in the direction of the grain with a wide, soft paintbrush, separated by ½" dry areas, which the stain may bleed over. Let dry for several hours or overnight. This is enough paper for one flower with a little extra left over.

2 When dry, stretch two of the strips out to 10" long, leaving the third strip unstretched to use later. Cut ten CHOC1 petals from the stretched paper and pleat the bottom ¼" of each with tacky glue, unstained side up. Each flower has eight petals, but prepare ten so you can pick your eight favorites in step 8.

3 Paint a light layer of solid red ink or watercolor in the direction of the grain on the unstained front face of each petal and let dry for about an hour.

4 Finely fringe a ½"-tall by 9"-long strip of outstretched paper cut from the reserved stained strip, leaving the rest unstretched. Save 2" of fringe for use in step 6. Hook the top of the stem wire down ¼", interlock the 7" of fine fringe, and wrap around the wire with tacky glue along the bottom, stained side in. Keep the fringe level while wrapping until the last 3", then step up ¹⁄₁₆" and finish wrapping, keeping level again.

5 Cut three ¾"-tall by 3½"-long strips of unstretched, stained paper with ½"-deep slits spaced a hair wider than ⅛" apart along each one. Set five individual segments from one strip aside to hold the tiny yellow florets. Create rolled fringe by rolling the segments on each strip onto themselves with tacky glue a few at a time between your thumb and forefinger. Fold the very top of each piece down and roll again to seal while the glue is still wet, creating rounded, slightly bulbous tips.

Finely fringe the tops of five ⅜"-tall by ⅛"-wide pieces of 100 gram yellow orange crepe paper and roll the bottoms to gather. Apply a light layer of tacky glue to the five individual brown segments and set a yellow tuft into each, the tops sticking up a little more than $\frac{1}{16}$" above the brown paper. Roll each brown segment closed, then open up the yellow fringe into tiny florets by rubbing across their tops with your finger.

6 Apply tacky glue to the bottom of each of the three rolled fringe strips. Wrap a longer piece around the fringed center, the rounded tops above the tips of the fringe a little more than $\frac{1}{16}$". Wrap the other longer piece up $\frac{1}{16}$" from the first, stretching a bit when needed to fill gaps in the first strip. Add the third, slightly shorter strip set down $\frac{1}{16}$" from the second strip, stretching to fill gaps as needed. Squeeze the bottom tightly to reduce the size and flare the top a bit. Tacky glue the five yellow floret pieces randomly around the center, their tips a hair above the adjacent rolled tips. Wrap the reserved 2" of fine fringe from step 4 around, level with the tips of the outer layer of rolled fringe. Squeeze the bottom again to secure.

Cut $\frac{5}{16}$"-deep slits spaced $\frac{1}{8}$" apart in a $\frac{5}{8}$"-tall by 2"-long strip of stained, outstretched brown paper, then cut a point in the top of each $\frac{1}{8}$"-wide segment. Apply tacky glue along the bottom and halfway up each point of the unstained side and wrap around the center once, the tips aligned with the rolled fringe tips. Cut away any excess, and bend each tip away from the center over a hat pin.

7 Dot red ink or watercolor over 75 percent of the rolled fringe tips. Lightly touch up the exposed sides of the fringe, the bent-back tips, and the outside of the whole assembly as well.

8 Lightly cup the center of eight petals. Turn the petal away from you and bend the top edge back with a nice round curve, then gently cup the back of each top side area, creating a petal that is concave in the center and convex around the top two-thirds of the perimeter. Most petals will be overstretched a bit at the top edges. Round the top corners and taper up toward the top tip of the petal slightly with sharp scissors.

CONTINUED

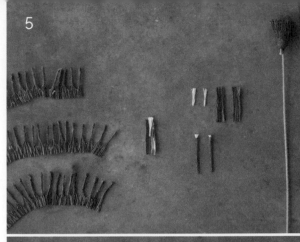

9 Bend the gathered base of each petal back ¼". Using hot glue on the bent base, carefully attach each petal to the flower's center, about one-quarter to one-third the way up the side. Smooth the petal ends down under the bottom of the base.

10 Locate the first three petals at the 12, 3, and 7:30 positions, staggering the fourth at around 6 o'clock. The petals should sit more or less horizontally, with the bases of the lower petals tight to the bases of the upper petals.

11 Position the next three petals at 1:30, 4:30, and 9 o'clock, followed by the final petal at 10:30. Following this order ensures the petals are placed naturally, instead of in a whorl, which you want to avoid.

12 Wrap the stem with outstretched strips of 100 gram green tea, limon, or yellow crepe paper. Create a simple calyx by cutting ⅛"-wide pointed and tapered segments into a piece of 1"-tall by 2"-long crepe in the same color as the stem. Wrap the calyx around the base with tacky glue. Let the glue set up for 5 minutes, then make a quick, slightly diluted stain by dipping your small paintbrush in the crimson watercolor or red ink, then into a small bowl of water, and paint the top and bottom of the calyx. Add a little color where the calyx meets the stem to soften that transition.

For a more realistic calyx, cut the inner calyx layer from outstretched stained red-brown crepe and an outer green layer in olive green doublette following step 7 of the Garden Cosmos tutorial (see page 102). Attach staggered with each other at the base of the flower.

garden cosmos

Tacky glue

180 gram #572 magenta
crepe paper

180 gram #600 white
crepe paper

180 gram #602
black crepe paper

180 gram #576
deep yellow crepe paper

180 gram #575
bright yellow crepe paper

180 gram #600/5
green-yellow ombré
crepe paper

Large paintbrush
(optional)

Wide, flat paintbrush

20-gauge green cloth-
covered stem wire

Leaves (see page 197)

Kitchen sponge (optional)

Water (optional)

Glass bowls (optional)

The garden cosmos is one of the simplest and daintiest in my cadre of paper flowers. Because of its delicate nature, just one bloom looks a bit flimsy for my taste, but en masse, garden cosmos can be a vision. They grow in a pretty range of pinkish purples, which can be re-created using different gradients of stain made from magenta-colored crepe paper. Staining your paper is optional, you can always skip the first two steps and stay with solid colors or plain white if you'd rather.

Garden cosmos centers can range from little pom-poms to flat discs ringed with fluffy, pollen-laden edges, so experiment with the sizes, shapes, and colors. A variety of centers can bring a wonderfully realistic look to your flowers, but centers made from the simplest yellow fringe are lovely, too. Outstretched 180 gram #562 dusty green crepe is also suitable for the outer calyx.

Another option for these simple flowers is to coat the petals with Mod Podge on both sides. The petals become diaphanous when they dry. Wait a half hour minimum for them to dry before creasing them. Tricks like this can transform cosmos from average to ethereal.

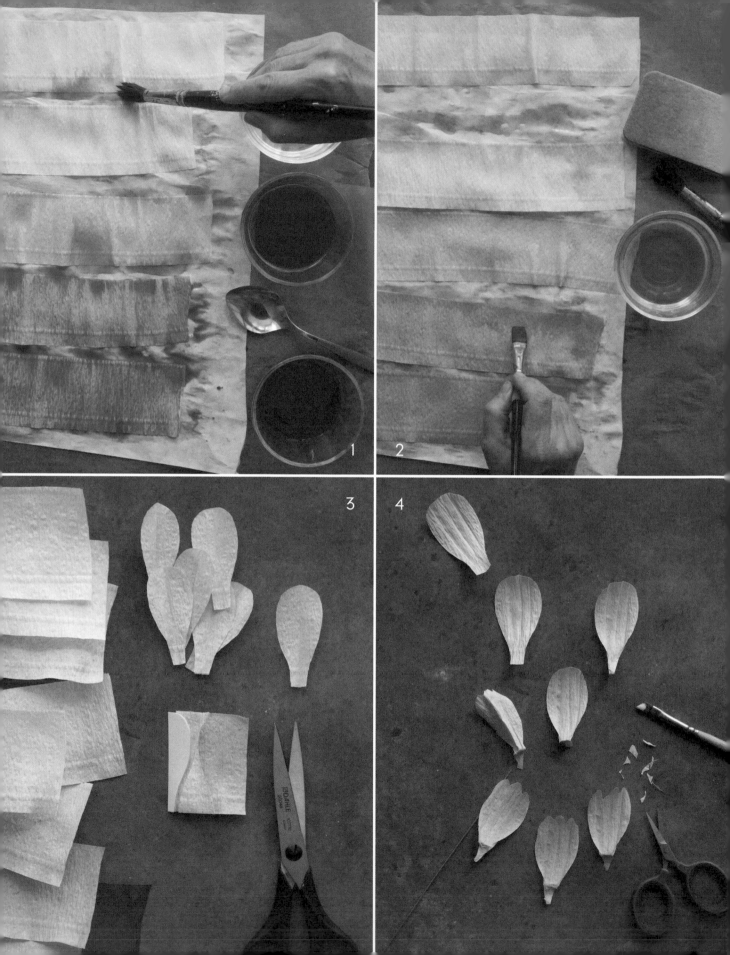

1 To create a range of colors for your cosmos, create a stain made from a 2" by 4" strip of 180 gram #572 magenta crepe paper soaked in ¼ cup warm water in a small glass bowl. Make a second bowl of diluted stain by pouring about one-third of the magenta stain into ¼ cup water. Keep a third bowl of clean water nearby.

Prepare as much paper as you would like to stain by cutting 2½"-tall by 9"-long strips of 180 gram #600 white crepe paper and outstretching them. You should be able to cut eight petals from each one. Be sure to include the fully uninterrupted portions of the paper between the machine lines for the upper parts of your petals so that the machine line is located near the petal base.

Lay the outstretched white crepe strips on a protected surface. Working evenly with a large paintbrush, paint some of the strips with the full-strength stain and some with the diluted stain. Wash others with plain water, running a small amount of full strength stain along the top or bottoms and letting the stain bleed into the water wash, creating an ombré effect.

2 Clean the large paintbrush, then use it to flood the stained strips while still wet with clean water to help even the color. Dab strips lightly with a sponge, then use a wide, flat paintbrush to mop away excess moisture. For the water-washed strips with just a touch of color, simply pat with the sponge to remove excess moisture. Let sit to dry, which should take 1 to 3 hours, depending on climate.

3 Select a color when the paper is dry. If using strips with color along one edge, decide if the color will be at the base or top of the petals, as it cannot be both on one flower. To make nicely symmetrical petals, select your petal size from the templates COS-Large or COS-Small and fold the template down its centerline. Fold and crease the stained paper with the color inward, and align the center fold of your petal template along it, the height of the petal running up and down the grain of the paper. Cut around the template and open up the petal. Repeat another seven times for one flower. If using plain, unstained paper, remember to outstretch the paper before cutting the petals.

4 To groom the petals, hold the base of each with the stained side up and pull your thumbnail up the center from base to tip to create a deep, strong crease. Repeat on either side of that crease, locating those creases slightly closer to the center than to the petal edges. Gather the bottom of each large cosmos petal by applying glue to the bottom ⅜", then folding each side of the bottom inward slightly to help pleat and taper the base of the petal. Bend the bottom ½" of the petal back, creating an area ¼"-wide at the fold where the petal will meet the flower. Take care that all of your petals are the same length before attaching to the center. If using the small cosmos petals, apply glue to the bottom ¼" and crimp to gather. The small petals also require a ¼"-wide area at the fold, so bend the bottom ⅜" back, adjusting the bend if more width is needed at the fold. Trim the tips into three or four bumps symmetrically about the petal's centerlines, remembering that you should not combine both types on the same flower. Create imperfections, if desired, by cutting irregular shapes into the tips or folding some petals downward along the middle crease. Consider leaving one or two petals out. Finish preparing your petals by lightly rolling the sides back over a hat pin.

CONTINUED

5 You will need 8" of laminated fringe strips for a smaller cosmos center and 15" for a larger one. Start by cutting ½"-tall strips of outstretched 180 gram #602 black ⅝"-tall strips of outstretched 180 gram #576 deep yellow and #575 bright yellow crepe paper at your desired length, either 8" or 15" long. Apply a layer of tacky glue to a strip of black paper and adhere it to a deep yellow strip with the top edge of the yellow paper ⅛" above the top edge of the black. Apply a layer of glue to the opposite side of the black strip, then adhere to a strip of bright yellow paper, aligning the tops of the yellow papers. Separate the two yellow layers with a hat pin to ensure they do not stick together. Create a few strips with just one layer of yellow paper over the black to use occasionally for variety. Let the strips set for 15 minutes. Finely fringe the strips along the unglued yellow edges when dry.

6 Create a ¼" hook at the top of the stem wire. For a larger, nickel-size, open cosmos center, interlock a 6" strip of laminated fringe with the hook, then glue and wrap with the bright yellow side in, keeping the top perfectly flat. Cut six 1½"-long segments from 9" of fringe. Tousle just the tiny yellow tips by gathering each segment together, pinching near the top, and rubbing your finger back and over the top. Glue two of the segments together at their bases with the tops aligned evenly, then glue the remaining four segments to the first two, deep yellow sides out, staggering each a hair down from the last. Glue the six segments together around the flat center, positioning the top 3/16" above the flat fringe. Trim as needed to fit. Squeeze tightly at the bottom until the glue sets. Fluff the fringe, grooming outward with a hat pin.

For a simpler, smaller center tuft, tousle the tips of 8" of laminated fringe and cut in half. Interlock a 4"-long strip with the wire, then glue and wrap with the light yellow side in, keeping

the top flat. Wrap the second 4"-long strip around, spiraling down just a hair at a time as you go. Fluff the fringe at the top and sides with a hat pin.

7 Glue the bent bases of two petals opposite each other at the center, ¼" down from the top, just below the yellow fringe. Attach a third petal between the first two, and then fill in between those with two more. Spiral the remaining three petals at the opposite side, each overlapping the next. Squeeze together at the base, and trim away excess petal bases below the flower center after glue has set.

For the inner calyx sepals, cut a 1"-tall by 1½"-long strip of outstretched crepe from the lightest part of a roll of 180 gram #600/5 green-yellow ombré paper. Fold over on itself eight times, crease the folds tightly and cut the sepals using guide COS-CLX1. Apply glue to the lighter side of the strip along the bottom and halfway up each sepal. Wrap around, stretching to position each sepal at the base of each petal. For the lower, outer calyx, cut a 1¾"-tall by 1¾"-long strip of slightly greener outstretched ombré crepe. Fold over on itself eight times, crease the folds tightly and cut the sepals using guide COS-CLX2. Glue and gather the bottom of the strip where the base meets the stem, spacing all eight sepals evenly. Glue down any flaps as needed, smoothing the transition to the stem with your fingers, and groom the sepals to curl down slightly. Wrap the stem to match or leave unwrapped.

8 Grow your garden of garden cosmos by trying color and size variations for the centers and petals. If making a full size cosmo leaf is too daunting, just a few tufts of green crepe paper slivers attached along the stem will do the trick.

5

6

7

8

poppies three ways

Tacky glue

Hot glue

Butter knife

Upholstery needle

Flat, stiff paintbrush

Light-green floral tape

16-gauge green cloth-covered stem wire

Leaves (see page 196)

OPIUM POPPY

180 gram #558 lime green crepe paper

180 gram #577 deep cream crepe paper

100 gram white crepe paper

180 gram #580 red orange crepe paper

Bleach

ORIENTAL POPPY

100 gram brown/gray crepe paper

180 gram #602 black crepe paper

180 gram #601 coral crepe paper (bleach dipped)

ICELAND POPPY

60 gram #296 yellow crepe paper

100 gram yellow orange crepe paper

100 gram green tea crepe paper

160 gram golden yellow crepe paper

Olive green crepe and crimson liquid concentrated watercolor for petal stain

Other assorted 100, 160, and 180 gram crepe papers for petal colors of your choice (optional)

Of all the paper flowers I make, poppies are the best served by color treating the crepe paper with a little dip in bleach or red or green stain to bring the petals closer to their natural color variations and hues. I use 100, 160, and 180 gram crepe papers for their texture and ability to hold the crumpled shapes of the petals and to take advantage of all the colors available across the three weights.

This tutorial covers opium, Oriental, and Iceland poppies. I have selected specific versions of the opium and Oriental poppies, namely the Danish Flag and the Coral Reef, but you can find these types of poppies in shades of purple and white as well. Iceland poppies can be made from your choice of a wide variety of colors, including red, white, beige, coral, yellow, tangerine orange, and pink.

Visualize petals as just having emerged from their small buds when crumpling them. Use the feathery edges of the Danish Flag poppy templates as a loose guide instead of trying to cut around them. Lay your floral tape pods over guides POD1 to 3 to get the right sizes and shapes, building them up quickly by folding the tape onto itself while stretching around the pods. Stems can be left unwrapped, unless attaching low-on-the-stem leaves.

1 Interlock floral tape through a ⅜" hook at the top of a piece of stem wire, then wrap tightly to create a pod. Use size guide POD1 for an opium poppy, POD2 for an Oriental poppy, or POD3 for an Iceland poppy, covering over the top ¹⁄₁₆" of the hook with tape.

For the opium poppy pod, use the blade of a butter knife, followed by an upholstery needle to score 12 radial furrows at the top of the pod. Cover with a piece of outstretched 180 gram #558 lime green crepe paper, gathering at the top. Slide the needle gently through the furrows to refresh them.

For the Oriental poppy pod, score 15 shallow furrows radially at the top of the pod with a butter knife followed by an upholstery needle, then stretch floral tape over the top and press the needle gently into the furrows to remold them. I like to leave the top of this pod green, but it also looks great covered with an outstretched piece of 100 gram brown/gray crepe paper. Wrap the sides with a strip of outstretched 180 gram #602 black crepe paper.

For the Iceland poppy pod, score six radial furrows in the top of the pod with a butter knife followed by an upholstery needle. Stretch floral tape over the top and remold with the needle. Glue a small circle of outstretched 60 gram #296 yellow crepe paper to the top, then immediately scrape the paper away in and around the furrows and make a small hole in the top with your needle, creating an amorphous yellow stigma shape.

2 For the opium poppy stamen, create two laminated fringe strips, each from a 1¼"-tall by 5"-long 180 gram #577 deep cream crepe strip tacky glued between two similarly sized strips of 100 gram white crepe, the cream layer ³⁄₁₆" above the white. Trim each to 1"-tall by 5"-long. Fringe the cream edge ¹⁄₃₂" wide (not finely) and ⅝"-deep. Bend the tips backward and let sit for 10 minutes, then tousle the fringe lightly to give it texture.

Apply tacky glue to the bottom of the strips and wrap a 1¼"-long segment around the pod, curving inward, aligning the tips with the top of the pod. The rest should bend outward around the base of the pod with the bottoms aligned and the upper tips sitting slightly lower than the top of the pod. Pinch the base to secure.

3 For the Oriental poppy stamen, create two laminated fringe strips, each from a 1¼"-tall by 6"-long brown/gray crepe strip tacky glued between two similarly sized strips of outstretched 180 gram #602 black crepe, the brown/gray layer ⅛" above the black. Trim each to ⅞" tall by 5" long. Fringe the brown/gray edge just shy of ¹⁄₁₆" wide and ⅝" deep. Bend the tips backward and let sit for 10 minutes, then gather and compress each strip lightly to tousle, avoiding the tips. Apply tacky glue to the bottom of the strips and wrap around the side of the pod with the inner tips ¹⁄₁₆" above the top of the pod, then downward in a slight spiral. Fluff with your finger when done.

4 For the Iceland poppy stamen, create one to three laminated fringe strips, each from a 1¼"-tall by 5"-long piece of 100 gram yellow orange crepe tacky glued between two similarly sized strips of outstretched 100 gram green tea crepe, the yellow layer ⅛" above the green. Trim each to 1⅛" tall by 4" long. Finely fringe the yellow edge ¾" deep. Bend the tips inward over a hat pin into tiny hooks. Bend the bottom ⅛" of the fringe strip back, then secure with hot glue around the bottom of the pod, hooks facing up. For a fuller stamen, tacky glue another one or two strips below the first, spiraling down slightly as you go. Open the fringe up almost horizontally and fluff the tips lightly.

1

2

3

4

5 For opium poppy petals, cut two inner OPIUM1 and two outer OPIUM2 petals from outstretched 180 gram #580 red orange crepe paper. To create the Danish Flag white cross, work in a well-ventilated area on a protected surface and apply bleach to only the area shown on the templates with light, dry brushstrokes on both sides of each petal. Let sit several hours until completely dry, then spindle the feathery edges lightly. Taking care not to rip the paper, stretch across the belly of each petal until it curves upward 90 degrees, then gather the bottom ½" in a pleat with tacky glue and bend back. These four petals should be uniform in profile.

For Oriental poppy petals, cut three inner ORIENTAL1 and three outer ORIENTAL2 petals from outstretched bleach-dipped 180 gram #601 coral paper. Accordion fold and spindle each petal onto itself and open back up carefully. Cup each petal, then style by leaving some parts upright with simple creases and crushing the sides or tops of others back over a wooden skewer. To create fallen pollen stains, rip three POLLEN RESIDUE shapes from outstretched black crepe paper. Apply a light layer of tacky glue to each black shape, press onto each of the three inner ORIENTAL1 petals where shown on the template and pull off immediately, leaving a grayish residue. Rip six BLACK BLOTCH shapes and tacky glue to the petals as shown on the templates, smoothing with your finger. Gather each petal bottom ½" in a pleat with tacky glue and bend back.

For Iceland poppy petals, create a stain from 2 drops of crimson liquid concentrated watercolor with a 2" square of olive green crepe paper in 2 tablespoons water. End-dip 160 gram golden yellow crepe paper in the stain and allow to dry. Lightly stretch the paper, then cut three inner ICELAND1 and two outer ICELAND2 petals. Accordion, spindle, and crumple each petal into

a ball, then open up wide enough to fill around the flower without losing all of the texture. The edges of these petals can be very crumpled, rolled back neatly on a hat pin, or left untouched. More pronounced creases can be made by pinching light lines of tacky glue up the back sides of a few of the petals. Gather the bottom ½" in a pleat with tacky glue and bend back.

6 For the opium poppy, attach the two inner petals (OPIUM1) directly opposite each other by applying hot glue to the tops, just above the folded bases, and pressing upward where the pod meets the stem. Trim off the excess paper at the bases, then apply the two outer cupped petals (OPIUM2) opposite each other in the gaps between the inner petals with tacky glue so that the four petals are evenly spaced. Trim off the excess paper, leaving a little extra to tacky glue down and create a clean intersection at the stem.

7 For the Oriental poppy, attach the three inner petals (ORIENTAL1) spaced somewhat equally around the bottom of the cylindrical pod with hot glue per step 6, obscuring the bottom of the stamen strips with the petals. Petals can overlap each other or partially cover the center of the flower, if desired. Attach the three outer petals (ORIENTAL2) staggered between the three inner petals with tacky glue, or leave one or two off for more movement. Trim and smooth the petals at the stem per step 6.

8 For the Iceland poppy, overlap the first two inner petals (ICELAND1) ½", with the third inner petal placed opposite that overlap, per steps 6 and 7. The two outer petals (ICELAND2) should be quite wide and placed opposite each other, bridging the gaps between the inner petals. Trim and smooth the petals at the stem per step 6. Older poppies will have petals that lay open with flatter surfaces, while younger poppies will have petals that are more unruly, crinkled, and cupped.

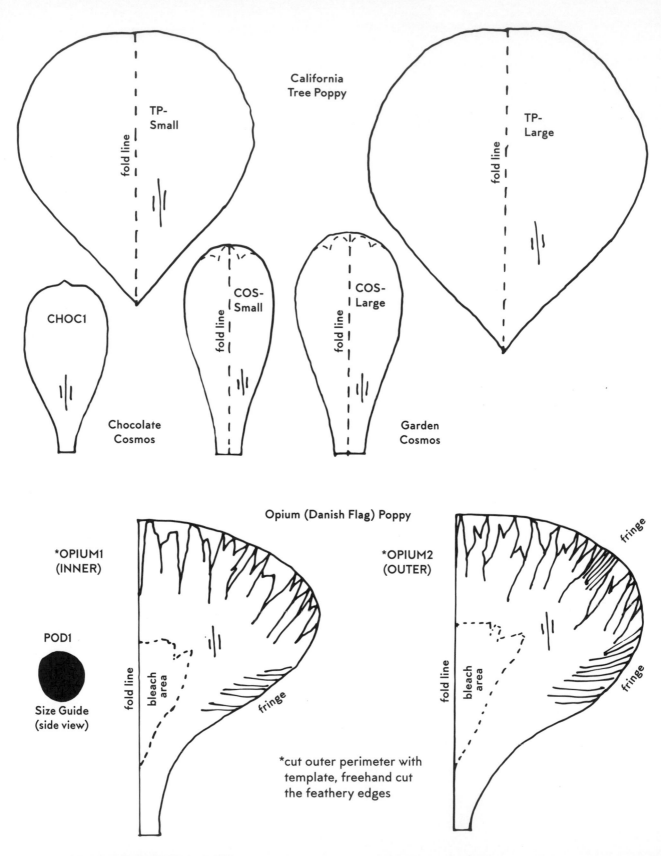

California
Tree Poppy

TP-
Small

TP-
Large

fold line

fold line

CHOC1

COS-
Small

COS-
Large

fold line

fold line

Chocolate
Cosmos

Garden
Cosmos

Opium (Danish Flag) Poppy

*OPIUM1
(INNER)

*OPIUM2
(OUTER)

fringe

fringe

fringe

POD1

fold line

fold line

bleach
area

bleach
area

Size Guide
(side view)

fringe

*cut outer perimeter with
template, freehand cut
the feathery edges

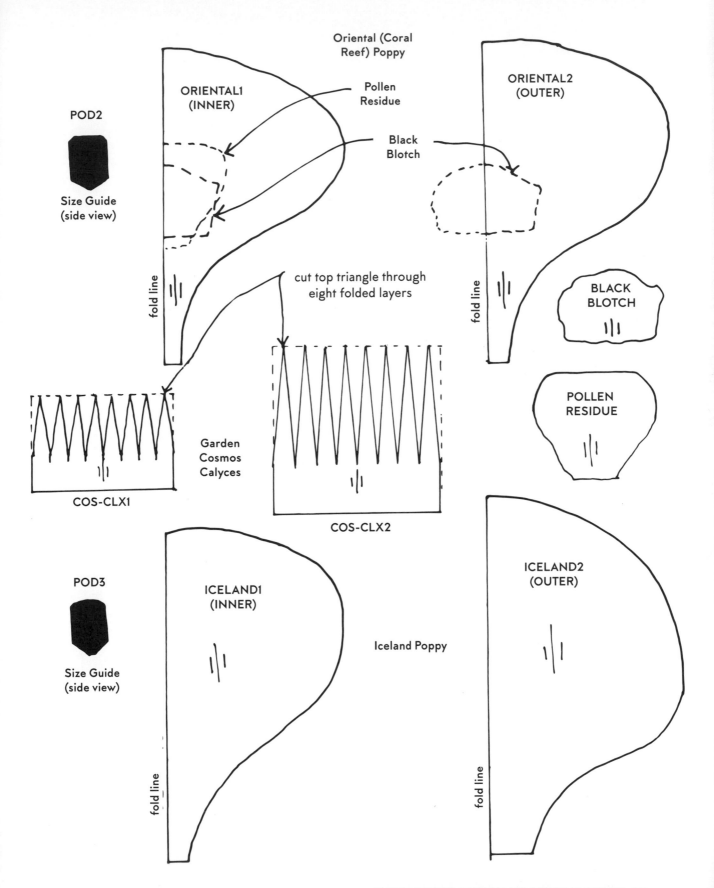

Oriental (Coral Reef) Poppy

POD2

Size Guide (side view)

ORIENTAL1 (INNER)

Pollen Residue

Black Blotch

ORIENTAL2 (OUTER)

fold line

cut top triangle through eight folded layers

BLACK BLOTCH

fold line

POLLEN RESIDUE

COS-CLX1

Garden Cosmos Calyces

COS-CLX2

POD3

Size Guide (side view)

ICELAND1 (INNER)

fold line

Iceland Poppy

ICELAND2 (OUTER)

fold line

candy striping & flecking

George Burns, Neil Diamond, Ferdinand Pichard, Jeremy Boldt, and Maurice Utrillo. These are not the members of some men's all-star team, but the names of some of the many candy-striped, flecked, blotched, and splashed flowers that exist today. In nature, candy striping and the like are the result of hybridization, viral infection, or genetic mutation and can be found on dahlias, zinnias, roses, peonies, carnations, morning glories, ranunculuses, and more. While not necessarily exotic, striped flowers are not something I see every day, and I absolutely adore them. I am not familiar with the meaning of most flowers, but I have read with amusement that a candy-striped carnation means "I'm sorry, I can't be with you," which is helpful to know, lest you give a striped carnation to the wrong person in your life.

Making candy-striped and flecked papers is simple and rewarding. The following pages demonstrate eight true-to-scale patterns and color combinations you can use for specimens in this book. Follow them loosely, keeping them irregular and unbalanced, and for the best, most natural results, cut your flower petals from the paper after you have applied the patterns and let them dry. Stretch the crepe per specific flower tutorials before striping and flecking, and adjust accordingly for petals taller than the patterns shown. Apply color to only one side of the paper using a small paintbrush and a toothpick for greater control. Cut the petals with their tips at the top edge of the patterns shown unless otherwise noted. To fleck paper, spray tiny color particles by running a protected thumb or forefinger away from the paper through the bristles of a stiff paintbrush dipped in the designated color.

candy-striping & flecking patterns &a papers

PATTERN 1 (Flecked)

Chabaud Picotee Fantasy Carnation

Paper: 180 gram ivory or light pink crepe paper

Color: Crimson liquid concentrated watercolor (also known as l.c.w.)

PATTERN 2 (Lightly Flecked)

Bristol Stripe Dinnerplate Dahlia

Paper: 100 gram white crepe paper

Color: Equal parts mahogany/crimson l.c.w.

Special Instructions: Add thin, elongated bits of flecking with a toothpick.

PATTERN 3 (Lightly Flecked)

Patricia Open-Centered Dahlia

Paper: Light yellow/yellow doublette

Color: Crimson l.c.w.

Special Instructions: See Pattern 2.

PATTERN 4 (Flecked)

Neil Diamond Hybrid Tea Rose

Paper: Pale pink/apricot doublette

Color: 8 drops crimson l.c.w. in ¼ tsp. water

Special Instructions: Cut petals from top and bottom edges of the pattern.

PATTERN 5 (No Flecking)

Carnevale Di Venezia Morning Glory

Paper: 180 gram #600/4 rose ombré crepe paper, cut from the center of the roll

Color: 2 drops alpine rose l.c.w. in 1 drop water

Special Instructions: Wipe a small paintbrush up and down the paper rapidly, making light, streaky brushstrokes with some gaps. Add tapered accent stripes and smatterings of thin, elongated flecks applied with a toothpick.

PATTERN 6 (No Flecking)

Pink Spinner Peony

Paper: 100 gram light pink or ivory crepe paper

Color: Alpine rose or crimson l.c.w.

Special Instructions: Treating each quarter of the 3" by 4" and 4" by 5" strips as a separate petal, brush a mixture of 4 drops concentrated watercolor in 1 tsp. water in watery streaks toward the center of each, leaving some almost bare. Add undiluted watercolor in random streaks down the petal centerlines or tapering inward symmetrically about them. When dry, cut petals one at a time.

PATTERN 7 (No Flecking)

Ranunculus Café variations

Paper: 160 gram golden yellow crepe paper

Color: Mahogany l.c.w. and black India ink

Special Instructions: End-dip paper strips in a mixture of 8 drops concentrated watercolor in 2 tsp. water. Brush a mixture of 1 tsp. water with 3 drops black India ink over the dipped edge and down in thin vertical brushstrokes from ⅛" to ½" apart and ½" to 1½"-deep. Add more brushstrokes of the black stain up from the bottom between the upper strokes, leaving some yellow exposed. Brush blotches of diluted mahogany here and there along the strip. Stain a small proportion of the paper with slightly undiluted mahogany watercolor. After the strip has begun to dry but can still wick moisture, run undiluted black ink along the top edge (not face) of the strip.

PATTERN 8 (Lightly Flecked)

Peppermint Stick Zinnia

Paper: 100 gram peach/beige crepe paper

Color: 3 drops crimson l.c.w in 2 drops water

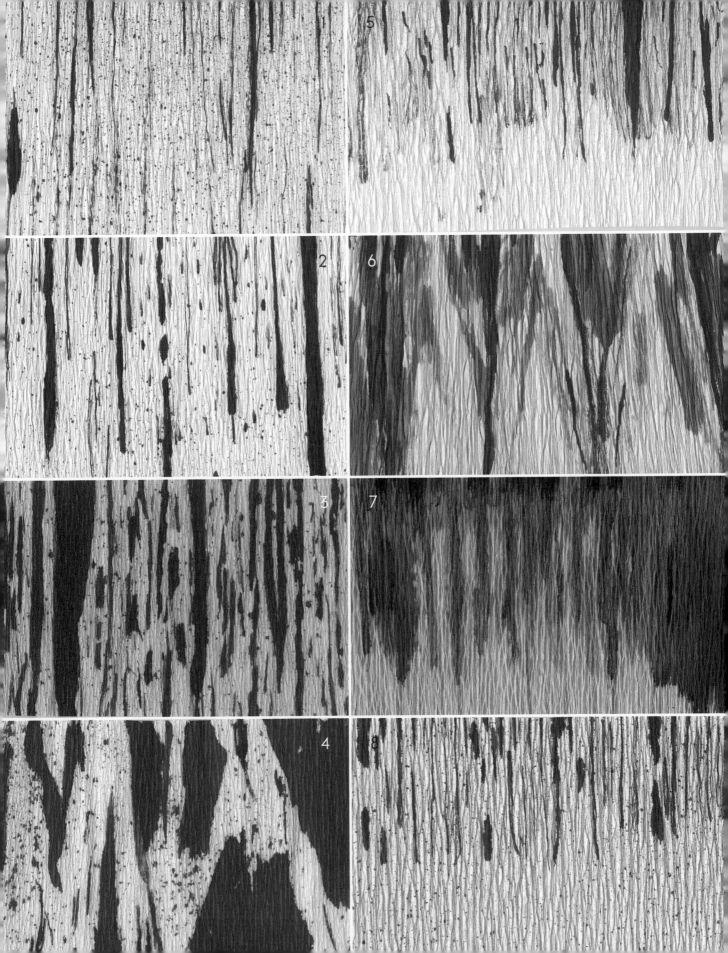

CONTINUOUS-STRIP FLOWERS

I am sentimental about this group of flowers. From the dandelion to the zinnias, most of them were cooked up during special times in my life, at artist residencies or when starting some of my first bridal designs or in the precious time of my life when I was walking my children to elementary school every day, finding inspiration along the way for things to make.

Assembling these flowers from continuous petal strips is quick work when you put it all together, but cutting the strips can be time-consuming. I think they are definitely worth the effort, even the poppies that are made from more than 14 feet of petals. The guides at the end of the section will show you how to cut each strip. Do not use them as templates. Instead, simply cut the lines shown on the guides into your precut and stretched strips of crepe paper, the sizes of which are prescribed in each tutorial.

These flowers are about as feathery as they get, and the colors run the gamut. I tried to provide a good range of color variations without causing too much confusion, but there are so many more colors to choose from. Remember to let the glue set as often as you can to keep your petal strips from sliding about while wrapping them around the base of your flowers.

dandelion

The real beauty of a paper dandelion is this: It won't wilt. Think of all the wildflower chains you've made that have lasted only about the time it took to weave them together. These will last much longer and can be woven into forever daisy chains, which are sure to be as enchanting as they are confusing to anyone who does not know they are paper.

Because of the way the double bract at the bottom of the flower overlaps the stem, it is best to start with a finished, waxy stem. It is important to pry the fringe and petals open horizontally after each step with gentle pressure to ensure your dandelions keep the proper form. When finished, randomly pinching a dozen petals at their tips and carefully slimming any petals that may look too wide with a pair of tiny scissors can give the flowers a more natural look. For slight variation from one dandelion to another, omit or add a petal strip as you go.

Find instructions on making a fuzzy, newly opened dandelion seed head on page 190 and a daisy chain on page 211 in "Things to Wear & Things for Your Hair." Paper dandelions also look great gathered in a vessel with several leaves tucked in among the stems.

Tacky glue

180 gram #576
deep yellow crepe paper

180 gram #575
bright yellow crepe paper

Olive green doublette
crepe paper

Light-green floral tape

Dandelion stem
(see page 190)

Leaves (see page 197)

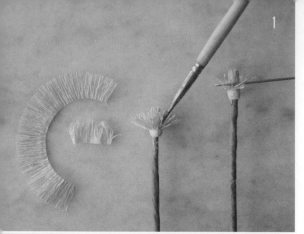

1 Stretch a strip of ⅝"-tall 180 gram #576 deep yellow crepe paper from 2½" to 4" long to thin it slightly. Finely fringe the strip, interlock with the stem hook, and carefully glue it around the wire. Keep the fringe level, raising the last ¾" up just a hair. Close the center of the fringe with a small dab of glue deep inside, then open up the outer layer and add light dabs of glue around the base. Smooth into a conical shape, keeping glue off of the tips for a more natural appearance.

Finely fringe a piece of ½"-tall by 1"-long piece of fully outstretched deep yellow crepe, and gently twist the strands to tousle. Glue the base around the conical center while stretching, positioning in such a way that the tips are level with the tapered center tip when pointing upward. Groom open with a hat pin.

2 Prepare a ¾"-tall by 12½"-long strip of TYPE A dandelion petals from a piece of fully outstretched 180 gram #575 bright yellow crepe paper. Cut into three 2½"- and one 5"-long segments. Additionally, finely fringe a ¾"-tall by 4¾"-long strip of outstretched deep yellow crepe. Cut into two 1"- and two 1⅜"-long segments, and create a small, visible hook along the top of each segment by folding the tips over a hat pin. Bend both the TYPE A and the hooked fringe strips back 90 degrees at the base, creating ⅛"-wide ledges for gluing, allowing the petals and fringe to radiate outward horizontally.

3 Glue the ledge of a 2½" segment of TYPE A petal strip from step 2 around the center just below the tousled fringe, stretching as you go. Stretch a 1" segment of hooked fringe just below that. Each segment of hooked fringe should match the length of the petals above it, so adjust accordingly as needed. Let set up for a minute, then groom the fringe and petals back outward, away from the tapered center.

4 Repeat step 3.

5 Repeat step 3, wrapping the petal strip without stretching. Use one of the two 1⅜"-long hooked fringe strips here.

6 Curve just the tips of the remaining 5"-long continuous strip of TYPE A dandelion petals from step 2 downward over a hat pin. Stretch them around the center, followed by the final 1⅜" segment of hooked fringe. Let set up for 1 or 2 minutes, then squeeze the base together and groom the layers open.

7 Prepare a ⅞"-tall by 9"-long strip of TYPE B dandelion petals from a piece of fully outstretched bright yellow crepe and bend the base back ⅛". Curve just the tips of the petals downward over a hat pin, then cut the strip into two 4½" lengths. Stretch one around the flower, making sure the petals are longer than the previous row by ¹⁄₁₆" or so, adjusting if they seem too long. Arc the petals on the remaining 4½" TYPE B strip downward slightly by pressing against the pad of your thumb and stretch around the flower. Use a hat pin to firmly pull and separate each layer back down. The inner, tousled bit of fringe around the center cone should splay outward, separated from the top petals.

8 For the layered bracts, start by cutting a series of ½"-deep slits ⅛" apart in a 1"-tall by 2"-long strip of olive green doublette. Trim each ⅛"-wide segment into a point with ever-so-slightly rounded sides. Apply tacky glue along the base and halfway up each of the pointed bracts on the more olive side. Wrap around the base of the dandelion with the tips sitting ¹⁄₁₆" to ⅛" shorter than the dandelion petals above them, fitting as many sepals as possible. Press the tips to the undersides of the petals to adhere, cutting away any extra.

For the smaller bracts, double over a 3"-long piece of light-green floral tape and cut a series of ⅛"-wide pointed sepals. Open back up and cut in half. Glue the base of one with its bottom ¼" below the underside of the flower, and the other ¹⁄₁₆" below that, staggering the tips. Cut away any extra, and cover any exposed stem below with light-green floral tape. Let dry for 10 minutes, then use a hat pin to bend the sepals downward and curl each tip back up.

echinacea supreme coneflower

Tacky glue

Hot glue

160 gram bright moss crepe paper

100 gram green moss green or 180 gram #600/5 green-yellow ombré crepep paper (bracts, stems, and leaves)

16-gauge green cloth-covered stem wire

Leaves (see page 197)

ECHINACEA SUPREME CANTALOUPE

180 gram #576/9 candy corn ombré crepe paper

Light salmon/light rose doublette crepe paper

ECHINACEA SUPREME MILKSHAKE

180 gram #576 deep yellow crepe paper

180 gram #577 deep cream crepe paper

180 gram #600 white crepe paper lightly tea-stained

100 gram ivory crepe paper

Have you ever seen such a comical flower as the Echinacea Supreme? They look like little jellyfish, and did you know that a group of jellyfish is called a "bloom"? Perfect. I have had my eye on this lesser-known coneflower for years, but as of this writing I have yet to actually hold one of those beauties in my hand. When I finally see one in person it will be like seeing a movie star—that's just how much of a fan I am.

This tutorial covers slightly different, interchangeable shapes for the centers and color combinations to make the Echinacea Supreme Cantaloupe and Milkshake, which are both stunners. If you are hungry for more, a little research can yield images of other coneflowers with fruity, fitting names like Marmalade, Meringue, Coconut Lime, Gumdrop, Pineapple, and Pomegranate, which can be made with simple adjustments to color and shape. The cones can vary from one flower to the next, so exaggerate the positioning of the layers of the fluffy petal strips to make a variety of profiles. Use the longer, drooping petals, as shown here, or the smaller ECH-Small petals, which can make this flower look literally as cute as a button.

If the head of your flower becomes at all wobbly while you are working on it, inject hot glue into the cavity at the base of the flower to secure it to the stem.

1 Create a twisted fringe strip by cutting one 1⅛"-tall by 12"-long TYPE C fringe from the end of a roll of 180 gram #576/9 candy corn ombré crepe paper for the Cantaloupe flower, or 180 gram #576 deep yellow crepe paper for the Milkshake. Twist each of the fringe pieces onto itself a few at a time with tacky glue, facing the orange out if using ombré paper.

Finely fringe a ¾"-tall by 14"-long strip of outstretched 160 gram bright moss crepe paper. Tacky glue to the twisted fringe ⁵⁄₁₆" down from the tips, covering the yellow side if using ombré.

2 For the Cantaloupe center, cut one 1⅛"-tall by 8"-long TYPE D petal strip from outstretched crepe from the center of the candy corn ombré roll. Cut six 1⅛"-tall by 12"-long TYPE E petal strips, three from light salmon/light rose doublette and three from outstretched candy corn ombré crepe at the section between 4⅜" and 5½" from the end of the roll.

For the Milkshake center, use the Cantaloupe strip dimensions to cut one TYPE D petal strip from outstretched 180 gram #577 deep cream crepe paper and six TYPE E petals strips from outstretched tea-stained 180 gram #600 white crepe paper.

3 Interlock the twisted fringe with a small hook at the top of the stem wire. Wrap around with tacky glue, green side in, keeping level and pointed upward. Squeeze the base frequently. Overlap the inner side of the last 3" of twisted fringe with the corresponding color TYPE D petal strip, set down ¹⁄₁₆". Wrap the TYPE D around the center with tacky glue, keeping level.

4 Layer the Cantaloupe TYPE E petal strips one at a time starting with two doublette strips, salmon sides up, both set ¹⁄₁₆" up from the TYPE D tips. Follow with the three candy-corn strips and the remaining doublette strip, rose side up,

stepping each down ¹⁄₁₆". Squeeze the base and bend the petals back after attaching each strip.

For the Milkshake TYPE E petal strips, follow the Cantaloupe instructions and position the top strip similarly, but step each of the five remaining strips down ¹⁄₁₆" from the one above, with the tea-stained sides facing up.

5 Bend the petals back over a skewer again, and brush them away from the center. Curve the tips of the bottom rows under slightly to help shape the center.

6 Cut 20 ECH-Large petals from salmon/light rose doublette for the Cantaloupe, or 100 gram ivory crepe for the Milkshake. Run your thumbnail several times up the front and then the back of each petal to bend it and give it some upward creases. Trim a small rounded V at the tip of each petal, then roll the bottom ⁵⁄₁₆" of each with tacky glue. The 100 gram paper stretches out more, so trim the top edges to taper slightly toward top if they become too wide.

Trim any loose paper away from the base before attaching the petals to the underside of the flower with tacky or hot glue on the bases and bottom ¼" of the petal faces.

7 Place petals around the flower in two irregular rows, with some petals barely overlapping each other and others in staggered pairs, leaving a few ⅛" gaps around the flower. Squeezing the base of the flower as you work pulls the two rows nicely out of alignment with each other. Petals can droop naturally or be bent down. The tips should always bend slightly inward.

8 Cut bracts from outstretched 100 gram moss green or 180 gram #600/5 green-yellow ombré crepe paper using guide ECH-BRCT. Wrap in a double layer at the base of the flower. Wrap the stem in outstretched green crepe of your choice, and match the leaves to the stem color.

eucalyptus

Tacky glue

180 gram #600 white crepe paper, lightly tea-stained

100 gram brown/gray crepe paper

180 gram #567 light brown crepe paper

Crimson liquid concentrated watercolor

Black coffee

Sturdy paintbrush with ⅛" rounded tip at handle

Light-green floral tape

20-gauge green cloth-covered stem wire

Bark paper (see page 55; optional)

Leaves (see page 197)

Eucalyptus might be a strange pick for a book on paper flowers, but I couldn't resist including them. These are loosely based on the nonnative blue gum eucalyptus tree pods that dot the paths in the Panhandle of Golden Gate Park, a place that is near to our home and dear to my heart. They possess the most beautiful hues of dirty white and waxy green when freshly fallen, which I've replicated here with tea-stained crepe paper and waxed floral tape. The palette of the leaves is just as pretty when dangling from the branches or fallen to the ground and dried to a crisp. I am not the first to take an interest in the eucalyptus pod and its form. If you ever get a chance to look at the incredible botanical glass works of Leopold and Rudolf Blaschka, you will be stunned by their fragile rendition.

As noted in chapter 1, the 100 gram brown crepe paper is actually an interesting shade of brownish gray. It is a nice color for the exterior of the pods, but you can use gray crepe or light-green floral tape as substitutes. This tutorial also calls for optional "bark paper" for dried pods and leaves.

1 Bend the top of an 8"-long piece of stem wire down 1½" and back up 1" to create a tight, S-shaped curve. Tie light-green floral tape around the wire at the top of the curve, then wrap tightly, building outward to ½" diameter. Occasionally spiral the tape down the stem ¾", but focus on the top, stretching and folding the tape over on itself to bulk up the pod faster. Keep the top surface flat, with the stem wire sticking up ⅜" from the center.

After the top portion reaches ½" in diameter, step down ⅛" and build the pod out to just shy of ¾"-diameter, then taper it down to a point on the stem ¾" below the flat top of the pod. Use EUC Eucalyptus Pod Guide on page 146 to check the size and shape.

2 Run the floral tape tightly across the top to smooth the surface. Pressing firmly with the rounded end of a sturdy paintbrush, make a continuous circular groove around the outer edge of the top surface, then rub six divots in the top, radiating from the center wire.

3 Stretch one ¾"-tall by 5"-long and one 1⅛"-tall by 5"-long strip of tea-stained 180 gram #600 white crepe paper to 9"-long to thin the paper somewhat. Finely fringe both strips. Wrap a ⅛"-tall strip of outstretched 100 gram brown/gray crepe paper once around the sides of the ⅛"-tall stepped portion of the pod base, adhering with tacky glue. Spindle the ¾"-tall strip of fringe and curve the tips inward over a hat pin. Apply tacky glue along the bottom of the strip on the same side as the curved-in tips and wrap around the brown/gray paper strip, taking care not to stretch the fringe while wrapping. The bottom of the fringe strip should sit on top of the ledge running around the pod. Smooth the fringe base to be sure it stays tight in the inset area of the pod.

4 Use a hat pin to pull back the fringe where it meets the pod at about a 10-degree angle all around.

5 Wrap a ¼"-tall strip of outstretched brown/gray crepe paper just below the bottom of the fringe cuts. If the brown/gray strip covers the step in the pod, press your thumbnail in and run it around to mark the step as a guideline. Spindle the remaining 9"-long fringe strip and curve the tips inward. Glue and wrap around the brown/gray paper strip, curved tips in, stretching as you go. The bottom of the fringe strip should align with the step, so when smoothed it is flush with the sides of the pod.

6 Groom the inner fringe layer out again, then separate the outer layer of fringe from the inner with a hat pin. Arc the outer fringe up and out by gently pulling between your thumb and hat pin. Trim a scant ⅛" off the tips of the outer layer with a slight bevel inward. Wrap the stem with outstretched 180 gram #567 light brown crepe paper, then wrap from the bottom of the fringe to the bottom of the base with outstretched brown/gray crepe.

7 If creating optional dried pods, follow step 1, but form smooth bases with ¾" diameter tops that taper down ¾" to meet the stem, without inset steps. Cover with outstretched bark paper, gathering the grain of the paper radially around the center wire at the top. Clip off the wire when done. Wrap stems as needed.

8 If desired, arrange stems with pods and leaves in clusters spaced 1" to 2" apart. Mix 1 drop of crimson liquid concentrated watercolor with 1 tablespoon of black coffee and dab along stems and pods to deepen the tone if desired.

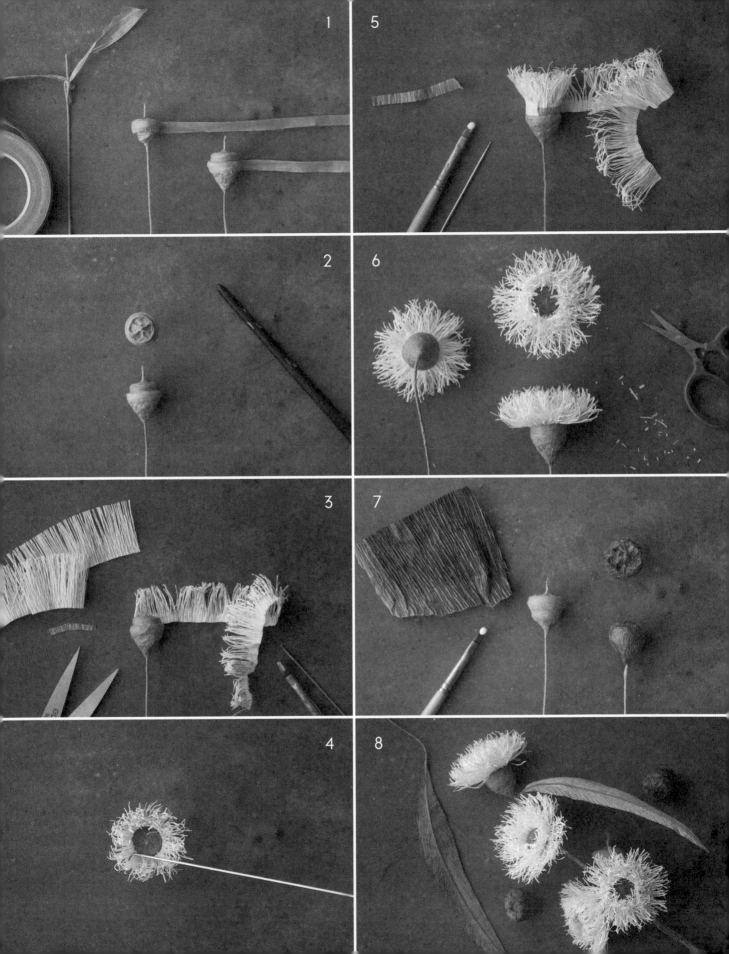

marigold

Paper marigolds are not hard to come by, as paper flowers go. The marigold is iconic, with its ruffled, dense, orange and yellow heads, so even when made with just a tuft of orange tissue paper atop a crude green stem, a paper marigold is unmistakable.

In my own work, realistic-looking life-size paper marigolds have been my white whale. A few years ago, I had a small solo show titled "One for You and One for Me," which featured two giant, 40"-diameter paper marigolds. I was very proud of that show, and somehow found those pieces easy, if very time-consuming, to create. But the small ones have really thrown me for a loop, until now. After what seems like one hundred test marigolds, I've finally found a solution. Continuous strips of rolled and ruffled petals wrapped around a skewer can be left in as a stem or removed, leaving a hole so the flower can be strung onto a garland. And while a little laborious, they don't take forever to make. Which is good, because there are some great ways to use them in chapter 4.

Wonderful 160 gram marigold crepe paper does the heavy lifting here, but try any 160 or 180 gram orange, yellow, or cream crepe, or use 180 gram #576/9 candy corn ombré crepe for interesting bicolored or ombré effects.

Tacky glue

160 gram marigold crepe paper

Olive green doublette crepe paper

Light-green floral tape

Bamboo skewer, 1 per flower

Leaves (see page 198)

1 Use the templates to cut eight TYPE F and eight TYPE G marigold petal strips from sixteen 1⅞"-tall by 6"-long strips of 160 gram marigold crepe paper that have been folded onto themselves eight times. Leave the bottom ⅛"-tall rim uncut to keep the petals connected. Cup the center of each petal on all sixteen strips.

2 For the eight TYPE F strips, wipe glue with a finger lightly onto the bottom ⅜" of each petal on a strip, then roll the base of the petal and the rim below it together from the backside between your thumb and forefinger, leaving the upper 1" of petal unrolled. Facing the petals away from you, hold one top corner and run your thumbnail across the back of the top edge of each, ruffling them and giving them a slight bend backward. Reroll each petal after ruffling, making sure the faces stay open.

3 Use a paintbrush to apply glue along the backside of the base of one TYPE F strip and gather around a skewer with the glue facing out. Squeeze the base very tightly, then apply glue to the inside of two more TYPE F base strips and wrap slowly, placing each petal facing inward around the flower, up ⅛" from the center. Most strips won't stretch all the way around the flower by themselves, so focus on the overall balance of the face of the flower. Dab glue into any loose flaps at the base, and squeeze underneath the petals as high as possible to round the flower and flare the petals outward.

4 Add three more TYPE F petal strips with glue along their bases and halfway up the face of each petal along the curved-in edges. Stagger them behind and between the previous strips, up another ⅛" to create a sunken center. Apply glue under loose bottom edges and flaps at the base after attaching, then squeeze and smooth down. Add the final two TYPE F petal strips similarly, up another ⅛", filling in around the flower as needed. Glue and squeeze the base tightly, as high as you

can underneath the petals, then slide the bamboo skewer out and back in to be sure it doesn't stick.

5 Repeat step 2 on the eight TYPE G petal strips, leaving the upper ¾" to ⅞" of each petal unrolled. With glue along the bottom strip and halfway up each petal face along the curved-in edges, wrap two TYPE G strips around with their bases ¼" below the point where the petals above angle out from the flower base, filling in as needed. Step down 1/16" with another pair of TYPE G strips around the flower, and again with the remaining two pairs. Squeeze the flower base as high and tight as you can. The bottom petals should sit horizontally.

6 Cut and cup 25 MAR petals. Roll the very bottom of each with glue, ripple the tops to bend back a bit as with the petal strips, and attach with ¼" glue, pressing up where the petals above meet the base, drooping down at the tips. Let dry, then trim the base to between 1" and 1¼"-long and wrap tightly with floral tape to sculpt a smooth, tapered calyx down to the stem.

7 For the calyx, cut two points into the top of a segment of floral tape and glue to the flower base with the tips bending outward underneath the petals. Repeat all the way around to cover the entire base, with 12 being the ideal number of points. Remove the skewer and trim the calyx tape neatly if using for a garland. If keeping on a stem, glue the skewer inside the flower, then wrap tape into a ⅜"-tall rounded nodule just below the calyx, projecting out 1/16" all around. Attach leaves as desired, and wrap the nodule and stem with outstretched strips of olive green doublette. Bend the skewer gently without breaking to give the stem a slight curve.

8 For a natural green tone at the center, make a stain with a 2" square of olive green doublette soaked in 2 teaspoons water and dab onto the innermost center petals. Let dry overnight.

the pom-poms

Tacky glue

Hot glue

GREEN TRICK DIANTHUS

160 gram olive crepe paper

100 gram green tea crepe paper

Flat, stiff paintbrush

18-gauge brown paper-wrapped stem wire

Leaves (see page 194)

LILAC POM-POM POPPY

180 gram #592 lilac crepe paper

180 gram #590 lavender crepe paper

100 gram green tea crepe paper

16-gauge green cloth-covered stem wire

Leaves (see page 196)

BLACK SWAN POPPY

180 gram #602 black crepe paper

180 gram #584 maroon crepe paper

180 gram #580 red orange crepe paper

Extra-sharp scissors

Modified opium poppy center and stem (see page 106)

Leaves (see page 196)

The first pom-pom flower I ever made was a Green Trick dianthus, a flower in the same genus as the carnation. It was part of a lovely wedding bouquet, and I made little green ball boutonnières to match. After that, all ball-shaped flowers began to catch my eye, especially the ones I've included here. The Lilac Pom-Pom poppy can be very true-to-life in paper. You can switch the paper color from lilac to red for a red pom-pom poppy, or to white for a frilly Swansdown poppy. The Black Swan poppy is an exotic specimen, at least to me. It borrows its center from another opium poppy shown earlier in the book, but when preparing it for the Black Swan, use only half of the laminated fringe stamen called for in the poppy tutorial. Feel free to add or subtract the number of petal strips and fringes in these tutorials to create variations from flower to flower. Remember, lopsided is almost never a bad thing.

If your flower heads begin to wiggle at any point, secure them to the stems inconspicuously with hot glue. The paper staining in the pom-pom poppy tutorials is optional. If you do stain the paper, be sure to plan ahead to allow time for it to dry. This is especially important for the Lilac Pom-Pom poppy, which is stained with the very wet "squeeze and soak" technique.

For an even more playful version of the Green Trick dianthus, see the boutonnières on page 213.

GREEN TRICK DIANTHUS

1 Create thirteen 1⅛"-tall by 12"-long strips of outstretched 160 gram olive crepe paper with a ripped top edge, and cut thirteen 1¾"-tall by 12"-long strips of 100 gram green tea crepe paper. Laminate the ripped strips to the bottom portion of the green tea strips with a thin layer of tacky glue applied with a flat, stiff paintbrush. Finely fringe the green tea edges ¾"-deep. Spindle the fringe on each strip.

2 Make 1½"-deep cuts every ⅜" along the fringed edge of each strip. Brush glue lightly on the green tea side at the middles of the ⅜"-wide sections, a few at a time. Pinch the green tea side closed, then roll each pinched section between your thumb and forefinger, creating a row of dark-green tubes with bright-green tufts. Roll each a second time to compact. Repeat along this strip, and on the remaining 12 fringe strips, staggering the gluing, pinching, and rolling for efficiency.

Cover the top 3" of the stem wire with a piece of outstretched olive crepe and hook down ½". Fold a rolled fringe strip onto itself with tacky glue along the bottom green tea side, hiding the green tea color inside. Interlock one end with the hook, then gather the strip tightly to form it into a fan-shaped wedge, thinner at the top and fuller at the bottom. Pull open carefully and dab tacky glue where needed to seal, then gather again and hold in place tightly until glue sets.

3 Form an additional 11 wedges, one at a time, resealing and tacky gluing each to the flower after forming. Squeeze each onto the last to adhere. Space wedges around evenly, allowing the bottom to undulate naturally, creating a wide, green globe. Secure in place with hot glue in the cavity at the base of the stem. Trim the last few wedges as needed to fit.

4 Tacky glue the final rolled strip, dark-green side facing down, to the bottom of the flower tight around the stem. Seal up stray flaps, then curve the tufts upward between your thumb and a skewer. Trim to shape and finish by wrapping the stem with strips of olive paper, adding sets of leaves if desired.

LILAC POM-POM POPPY

1 Cut ten 1¾"-tall by 12"-long strips from outstretched 180 gram #592 lilac crepe paper. Stain the top edges of three strips with 180 gram #590 lavender crepe paper using the paper-on-paper staining "squeeze and soak" method on page 55. When dry, cut the seven unstained and two stained strips into TYPE H petal strips, the two stained strips cut along their stained edges. Reserve the final stained strip for use in step 4.

Spindle a 1"-tall by 2"-long strip of TYPE I fringe strip cut from outstretched 100 gram green tea crepe paper. Loop the top of the stem wire down ⅜", interlock with the strip, and wrap around the loop with tacky glue, with the green tips ½" above the loop.

2 Spindle five unstained strips of the TYPE H petals. Unfurl and apply tacky glue to the ½" uncut bottoms of each of the strips. Wrap each strip around tightly, aligning the bottoms, with the top of the first strip ¾" above the wire loop. If the tuft rides up the stem, press your finger into the center and push it back down. When all five strips are attached, smooth the base and let them set up for 10 minutes.

3 Spindle only the tops and bottoms of the remaining four unstained and two stained strips of TYPE H petals, leaving the midsections untwisted. Unfurl, then one at a time apply tacky glue and wrap the strips around the base of the flower, saving the two stained petal strips for last. Wrap in the elbow where the vertical base and the horizontal petals meet, so the bottom strip will conceal the base and the lowest petals will lay horizontally. Groom the bottom layers to droop downward slightly with your fingers.

4 Cut four petals using the POMPOM1 template from your final strip of stained paper with the color at the tips facing either up or down. Cup the centers of each petal across the middle to widen, and droop the ends down by pulling between a skewer or hat pin and your thumb. Equally space the petals around the base, attaching to the underside of the poppy near the stem neatly with a ¼" bead of hot glue at the base of each petal.

BLACK SWAN POPPY

1 Using the paper-on-paper staining technique shown on page 55, overlay a 1¼"-tall by 8"-long strip of unstretched 180 gram #602 black crepe paper along the bottom half of a 3½"-tall by 10"-long strip of outstretched 180 gram #584 maroon crepe paper. Let dry and set aside for use in step 8.

Cut 15 TYPE H 1¾"-tall by 12"-long pom-pom petal strips from outstretched maroon crepe paper, six 12" strips and one 6" strip from outstretched black crepe, and a 6" strip from outstretched 180 gram #580 red orange crepe paper. Finely fringe a 1¾"-tall by 9"-long strip of outstretched red orange crepe and a 1¾"-tall by 6"-long strip of outstretched black crepe, leaving ½" of uncut paper at the bottom of each.

2 Adhere the 6" strip of red orange TYPE H petals to one end of a full strip of maroon petals with tacky glue along the uncut bottom, then layer the 6" strip of black fringe over that. Add tacky glue to the remaining 6" of maroon and fold over, making a sandwich with the maroon paper at the outside. Fold this strip over onto itself with the black toward the center, tacky gluing together along the bottom, creating a 3"-long row of petals that will be located closest to the poppy's center. Repeat using a second full strip of maroon petals sandwiching 6" of the red fringe layered with the 6"-strip of black petals. Fold and secure with black petals toward the center. Spindle both folded pieces firmly when set up a bit.

3 Apply tacky glue along the bottom of the first 3" row of petals from step 2 and wrap them around the poppy center, with the tips ½" above the center, tilting slightly outward. Pinch the bottom after wrapping and cut away excess damp paper. Cut ⅛" from the bottom of the second row of petals from step 2. Tacky glue around the first row of petals, keeping the tips at the same height as the first row. Squeeze the base together tightly as the glue starts to set up.

4 Sandwich the remaining six 12"-long black TYPE H strips between twelve 12"-long maroon TYPE H strips with tacky glue along their bottoms. Randomly glue bits of the remaining 3" of red orange fringe on each, let sit for 5 minutes, then spindle and unfurl. Fold one of the maroon-and-black strips into thirds and secure together with hot glue at the bottom faces. While the glue is still warm and pliable, carefully gather the bottom to create a tapered fan shape. Trim ⅛" from the bottom and then attach to the flower head with ½" hot glue, with the most inward petal tips at the same height as the previous row. This first segment should span one-third of the way around the flower.

5 Fill in around the flower with two more fan-shaped segments per step 4. Add to the natural appearance of the poppy by leaving a small gap between two of the segments.

6 Repeat step 4 to make three final fan-shaped segments. Gather them as much as possible at the bottom to help them fan out axially when placed around the flower. Trim a curved ¼" from the bottom of each segment, and trim the bottom corners of each off at an angle. Attach each with hot glue along the bottom ½" and along the cut end, adding extra glue as needed. The poppy head should now be roughly 2¼" from center to tip of the bottom petals, in a gradual curve down from the top.

7 With a pair of extra-sharp scissors oriented vertically, cut into the poppy head quickly ten to fifteen times to give it a more irregular appearance. Using tacky glue, wrap the final maroon TYPE H petal strip around the base to cover the bottoms of the petal segments.

8 Cut four petals using the POMPOM2 template from the reserved strip of black-stained paper with black tips facing up. Cup the center of each petal across the middle to widen, then spindle, unfurl, and droop the ends down by pulling between a hat pin and your thumb. Attach to the underside of the poppy with a ½" bead of hot glue at the base of each petal, equally spaced and touching the stem.

zinnias two ways

Tacky glue

Hot glue

100 or 180 gram moss green
crepe paper

Olive green doublette
crepe paper (washed with
water and dried; optional)

Light-green floral tape

18-gauge brown paper-wrapped
stem wire

Leaves (see page 198)

BENARY'S GIANT ZINNIA

180 gram #566 pale green
crepe paper

160 gram light salmon
crepe paper

100 gram peach/beige
crepe paper

Any bright-yellow crepe paper

Toothpicks

SCABIOSA-FLOWERED ZINNIA

100 gram scarlet crepe paper
(or maroon crepe paper
of any weight)

180 gram #577 deep cream
crepe paper

160 gram light salmon
crepe paper

100 gram peach/beige
crepe paper

180 gram #569 pale pink
crepe paper

It is rare to find a paper zinnia, I think. I hadn't seen one before I made one myself, but now they are some of my very favorite paper flowers of all. Zinnias are such excellent specimens to let you take advantage of the varied range of colors and types of crepe paper. Both the Benary's Giant and Scabiosa-flowered zinnia strains feature iconic, bright, single-color heads as well as subtle, antique-looking two-toned blooms. The Scabiosa-flowered zinnia is fuzzy and a little silly looking, sort of like a Sno Ball, and a little bit obscure, sort of like an Echinacea Supreme.

Note that the Scabiosa-flowered zinnia center can be used for any of the Benary's Giant zinnias as well. If using 160 or 180 gram crepe paper for the petals of either flower type, stretch your paper as far as you can between your hands easily and without forcing before cutting the petal strips, but 100 gram crepe can be used as is. The final few strips of petals for the Benary's will need to be hot glued up to the underside of the petals above them in order to position them correctly. It is nice to give the petals an extra curl under at the tips when the flower is finished, but it is not required. The petal crimping technique on the inner Benary's petal strips is a little time-consuming, but worth it.

1 Cut thin ½"-tall points close together along a ¾"-tall by 8"-long strip of 180 gram #566 pale green crepe paper. Curve the points inward just slightly over a hat pin, hook the top of the stem wire down ¼", and interlock the strip with the hook. Tacky glue the strip around the wire with the curved side in, wrapping without stretching. Keep the first 3" level, then spiral the remainder up very gradually. Pinch the green tips together, pushing downward at the same time to shape, then squeeze the base together tightly.

2 Cut one ⅞"-tall by 3"-long strip and two 1⅛"-tall by 3½"-long strips from 160 gram light salmon crepe paper that has been stretched as far as you can without forcing it. Cut ⅝"-deep slits ⅛" apart along the smaller strip and a hair farther than ⅛" apart on the larger strips. Pull the corner of your thumbnail up each petal segment from base to tip on all three strips, causing the edges to curl inward. Round and slightly taper the petal corners on all three strips with tiny scissors and set a larger one aside for use in step 3. Wipe tacky glue with a toothpick into the base of each petal on the other two strips, crimping each base closed around the toothpick before you slide it out. Keep the petals facing up.

3 With tacky glue along the bottoms, wrap the tips of the smaller crimped strip ¹⁄₁₆" above the pointy center, followed by the slightly larger crimped strip up ¹⁄₁₆" from the first. Adjust the petal placements to fill gaps as needed. Switch to hot glue and attach the reserved uncrimped petal strip from step 2 up ⅛" from the inner petals, the ends of the petals curving outward, then groom all the petals down a bit.

4 Cut one 1"-tall by 6"-long and four ⅞"-tall by 9"-long strips of unstretched 100 gram peach/beige crepe paper. Cut ¾"-deep slits ³⁄₁₆" apart in the 6" strip and the first 9" strip, and ¼" apart in the three remaining 9" strips. On all five petal

strips, round and slightly taper the corners of each petal, then pull the ends between your hat pin and thumb to curve them and widen the ends a bit. Gently cup the undersides of the petal tips on one of the strips with the ¼"-wide petals to make them slightly wider than the others and use last in step 5.

5 Using hot glue, wrap the 6" strip first, followed by the 9" strip with the ³⁄₁₆" petals and one with the ¼" petals, each ⅛" higher than the last and wrapped level with itself twice before spiraling up slightly. Groom the petals downward to sit horizontally, then attach the final two petal strips to be just a hair longer than ones above them, no more, no less. Groom the petals down and away from each other when finished.

6 Cut a few ⅛"-wide by ½"-tall tiny teardrop shapes from the light salmon and any bright-yellow crepe. Cup each one, gather the bases, and tacky glue them irregularly near the light green center of the flower to give it a more natural appearance.

7 Build the calyx up with floral tape to around ¾"-wide just below the flower, and taper down smoothly around ⅞" to the stem. Finish the calyx with olive green doublette per step 7 of the Scabiosa-Flowered Zinnia on page 145.

8 For two-toned zinnias, feel free to extend the inner color to the first petal strip of step 4 for variety. Other perfect zinnia petal colors include 180 gram #558 lime green, 100 gram peach/beige with #600/4 rose ombré, 100 gram hot pink with 100 gram dark pink, pale pink/apricot doublette, and my favorite, candy-striped. Find more on candy striping on page 114. The leaves for both this and the scabiosa-flowered zinnias are some of the most unique in the book. I suggest you try them!

SCABIOSA-FLOWERED ZINNIA

1 Finely fringe a 1"-tall by 5"-long strip of unstretched 100 gram scarlet crepe paper and hook the tips over a hat pin. Glue a scarlet scrap to the stem wire and hook it down ¼". Interlock the fringe ⅛" above the hook and apply tacky glue to the bottom. Spiral up around the wire very gradually, setting the hooks just above the ones below them, creating a ¼"-deep center recess. Finely fringe a 1"-tall by 6"- to 8"-long unstretched strip of 180 gram #577 deep cream crepe. Lightly spindle and curve the tips in subtly. Apply tacky glue and wrap loosely ⅛" above the scarlet center, keeping the center recess open.

2 Cut four 1"-tall by 6"-long strips from 160 gram light salmon crepe paper that has been stretched as far as you can without forcing. Cut four similarly sized strips from unstretched 100 gram peach/beige crepe paper and five from fully outstretched 180 gram #569 pale pink crepe paper. Always cut the bottom five strips of this flower from outstretched crepe.

Cut a series of ¾"-deep slits in each petal strip spaced ⅛" apart in the first two salmon strips, $\frac{3}{16}$" apart in the second two salmon and first peach/beige strip, ¼" apart in two more peach/beige strips, and $\frac{5}{16}$" apart in all remaining strips. Round and taper the petal corners and cut a ⅜"-deep slit down the center of each by following petal guides SFZ1 to 4. Trim all the petal corners on one side of the petals, flip over and trim the opposing corners, then cut the center slits. Pull the tips of the petals between your hat pin and thumb to widen a bit.

3 Gather and softly twist each strip in one direction. Working from thinnest to thickest petals, keeping each strip level with itself, tacky glue the first salmon petal strip $\frac{1}{16}$" above the deep cream fringe, then the remaining three salmon petal strips each $\frac{1}{16}$" above the one before it.

4 Tacky glue the four peach strips around the salmon strips, the bottoms aligned with the last salmon strip. Use a hat pin to groom the petals downward.

5 Use hot glue to attach the five pink petal strips. Wrap three with their bottoms aligned with the last peach strip, then glue the final two strips to the underside of the base, the bottom of each $\frac{1}{16}$" inward from the one above it. Fluff all of the petals downward firmly with your fingers.

6 Fill the bottom cavity with hot glue. Cut 16 SFZ5 and 8 SFZ6 skirt petals from outstretched pale pink crepe. Crease up the center of each SFZ5 and curl the tips upward with your thumbnail. Pull your thumbnail along the back of each SFZ6 several times to cup and curl downward. Gather the bottom ½" of each with tacky glue. Attach the petal bases to the underside of the flower pointing horizontally or downward, extending out ½" past the petal strips above them. The petals can overlap or have gaps between them, with several of one type in a row or in a random order.

7 Build up a floral tape calyx, tapering from ⅝"-wide at the flower base down ⅞" to the stem. Cut a series of ½"-deep slits a little over ⅛" apart along a strip of ⅞"-tall by 8"-long olive green doublette. Round the top of each sepal segment, then tacky glue the base and sepals in one layer around the bottom of the flower to cover the skirt petal bases, followed by a second and third layer each staggered $\frac{1}{16}$" below the first. (On a Benary's zinnia, set the sepal tips closer to the base of the flower.) Wrap the bottom of the calyces and stem with outstretched moss green crepe.

8 These zinnias grow in ombré sunsets perfect for a nuanced roll of candy corn ombré crepe, puffs of purely pale peach, and dozens of two-toned pastel combinations, my favorite being light pink at the interior with pale pink outer petal strips and flirty skirt petals.

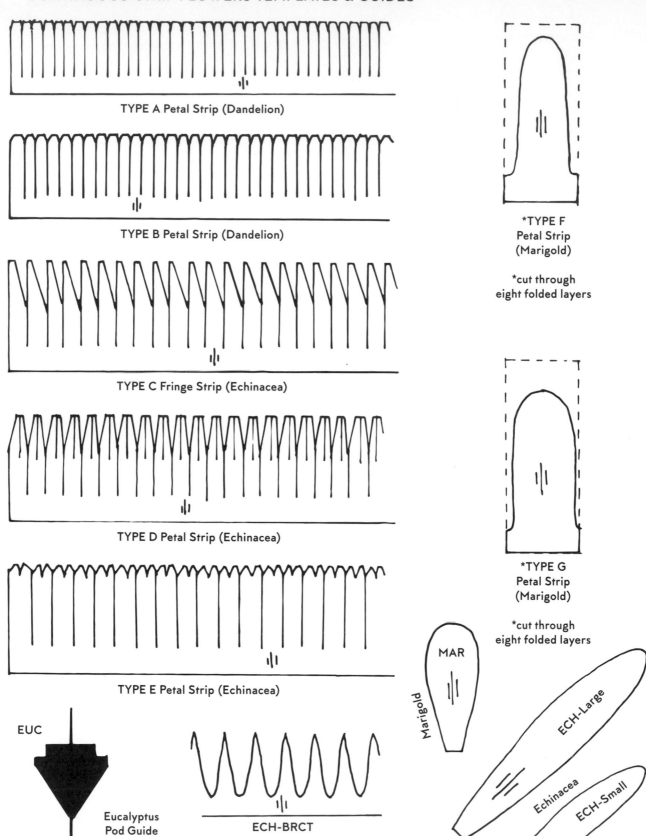

TYPE A Petal Strip (Dandelion)

TYPE B Petal Strip (Dandelion)

TYPE C Fringe Strip (Echinacea)

TYPE D Petal Strip (Echinacea)

TYPE E Petal Strip (Echinacea)

*TYPE F
Petal Strip
(Marigold)

*cut through
eight folded layers

*TYPE G
Petal Strip
(Marigold)

*cut through
eight folded layers

EUC

Eucalyptus
Pod Guide

ECH-BRCT

Echinacea Bract

MAR

Marigold

ECH-Large

Echinacea

ECH-Small

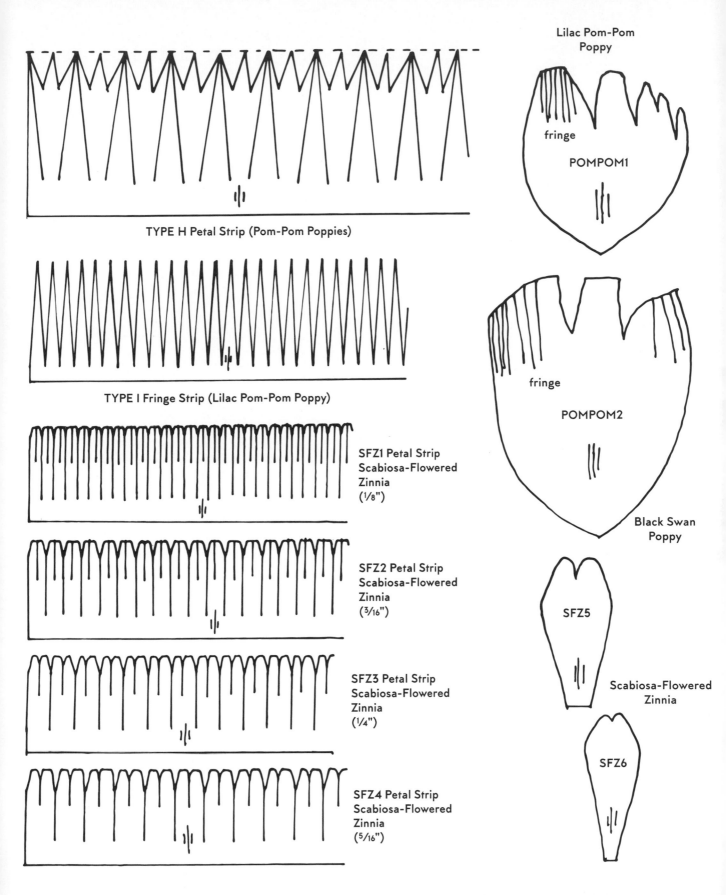

TYPE H Petal Strip (Pom-Pom Poppies)

TYPE I Fringe Strip (Lilac Pom-Pom Poppy)

SFZ1 Petal Strip
Scabiosa-Flowered
Zinnia
(1/8")

SFZ2 Petal Strip
Scabiosa-Flowered
Zinnia
(3/16")

SFZ3 Petal Strip
Scabiosa-Flowered
Zinnia
(1/4")

SFZ4 Petal Strip
Scabiosa-Flowered
Zinnia
(5/16")

Lilac Pom-Pom
Poppy

fringe

POMPOM1

fringe

POMPOM2

Black Swan
Poppy

SFZ5

Scabiosa-Flowered
Zinnia

SFZ6

imperfections & wilt—dead paper flowers

Capturing the state of botanicals in decay is something I pursue in my fine art practice. Decomposing flowers speak to me, not only with their reminder of this temporary thing called life, but also in the imbalance of their actual physical composition. There is so much movement in a flower as it falls apart and loses its symmetry, and a beautiful tension in a flower that is hanging on as long as it can. Have you ever seen a poppy just before it loses its petals? The petals bend so far down in such a tremendous gesture of shoulders-back, chest-up surrender that it stops my heart.

Who wouldn't want to try to capture these gestures in their work? The opportunity for experimentation and artistic license in the portrayal of dying flowers is huge. Art and decay have gone hand in hand forever, and the art of paper flower making specifically lends itself to depicting imperfections and wilt due to its three-dimensionality. I find making a dead or dying paper flower as compelling as any other.

With a few exceptions, I do not like to apply decay or wilt, opting instead to build my dead flowers one petal at a time. Following are some ideas to turn your flowers perfectly imperfect.

OBSERVATION

For your own edification, it is important to observe how real flowers fall apart. Note what remains of the stamens, the shapes petals take when drying out, and if parts of a flower keep their color or not. Note the posture of the stems and neck, and the position of individual petals. A rotting dahlia's petals will collapse down over its face like a sad lion's mane, while a rose might stay erect, only its texture and colors changing. A peony head set square on a table will shrivel in the middle while it melts into the table and its ends curl up. The forms created by abnormal growth such as fasciation and phyllody are fascinating and fantastical, too, and worth looking into.

PAPER COLOR

White crepe paper stained along the edge with strong black tea is fitting for fading flower petals, allowing you to cut petals that are brown at the tips and top edges but still have fresh faces. Crepe washed in larger swaths of tea takes on an irregular brown tone that works well for flowers whose petals fade all at once. For flowers like dahlias that deepen in color as they wilt, use coffee in small amounts on bright-colored doublette to create dirtier, darker versions of those colors. For a completely desiccated flower, outstretched 180 gram #567 light brown crepe is an exact match. Use 180 gram #562 dusty green crepe for old leaves. It lacks pigment in a way that already seems faded and withered.

PAPER TEXTURE

Use the crushing technique on page 23 to give petals a crumpled texture when needed. Do not be afraid to pinch, roll, fold, or cut rips in your petals. If a flower dies on the ground, gravity will have its way with the flower and it will deflate. So, occasionally, after I have constructed an entire wilting flower, I will go one step further and actually step on it.

PETAL BY PETAL—DAHLIAS & OTHER BEAUTIES

A few of the real showboats and prizewinners live in this part of the book. Dahlias and peonies come in so many sundry specifications that it can be maddening to try to know them all. I offer a small range of them here, and they are really the most impressive paper flowers when made with care.

When working on dahlias and ranunculuses, it is important to try to avoid the look of assembly-line production, which is why in some cases I walk you through the petal placement, similar to the rose tutorials. We are again looking for those little missed beats and doubled-up elements that are found in nature. After you have tried a few of these tutorials, do some garden or farm research to explore the multitude of sizes and shapes and colors these flowers come in, so as not to be limited by what I've demonstrated here.

I have been known to spend a full day on a ranunculus and two days or more on a dinnerplate dahlia. This is because I tend to work hard, not smart. I have endeavored to boil these tutorials down to the smartest directions possible, which has included making the petals all at once, as opposed to three at a time, as I am wont to do. Some of these tutorials might take a little more time than average, but the results will be spectacular, I promise.

dinnerplate dahlia

Tacky glue

Hot glue

180 gram #600/1 raspberry ombré crepe paper

100 gram peach/beige crepe paper

180 gram #600/5 green-yellow ombré crepe paper (inner sepals)

Olive green doublette crepe paper (outer sepals)

Wide, firm paintbrush

24-gauge white cloth-covered stem wire

Crimson liquid concentrated watercolor

Old kitchen towel

Light-green floral tape

18-gauge brown paper-wrapped stem wire

Leaves (see page 198) and buds (see page 190)

Mod Podge (optional)

I'm a big fan of dahlias, and it's a nice walk from our place to the Dahlia Garden in Golden Gate Park, where we can watch them start to pop up in June and July and then explode into a kaleidoscope of color later in the summer. Some of my first large-scale fine art pieces were giant paper dahlias. I love the featherlike quality of the petals and their incredible patterns and colors. Dinnerplate dahlias are some of the most spectacular, due to their enormous size, and I don't know anyone who doesn't swoon over a Café au Lait dinnerplate dahlia, with its delicate tone and sometimes irregular, wavy, swirling petals.

Dinnerplate dahlias are exquisitely suited for bridal bouquets, as shown on page 217. They also can be built on a simple base to make the ultimate flower fascinator, as described on page 223, and can offer structure and dazzle to larger headdresses, as shown on page 226.

I prefer to make my dahlias slightly recessed at the center instead of making an inner bud cluster of petals. I love to place several swirling and curling petals around the center, but you can omit those if you'd like. Other colors like 100 gram ivory crepe or Bristol Stripe Pattern 2 on page 114 can be used instead of the Café au Lait colors specified. These paper dahlias reach between 6 and 7" in diameter, but can grow up to 10 to 12"-wide in real life.

1 Hook the top of the stem wire down ¼", interlock with floral tape, and wrap tightly into a ⅝"-diameter ball. Tacky glue a scrap of raspberry ombré crepe paper to the top. Cut three 1½"-tall by 4"-long strips from the area located between 5½" to 7" from the end of a roll of 180 gram #600/1 raspberry ombré crepe and one from 100 gram peach/beige crepe, both papers having been stretched between your hands as far as you can without forcing. Fold each 4" strip in half three times and cut a tall triangle, leaving ¼" uncut at the bottom, then cup each triangle. The tips should be lighter and the colored sides convex on the raspberry triangles. One at a time, tacky glue two raspberry strips around the ball, bottoms aligned with the bottom of the ball. Tacky glue the peach/beige strip staggered inside the remaining raspberry strip, then glue around the ball with bottoms aligned. Pinch the tips inward a bit.

From similarly stretched paper, cut nine peach/beige and three raspberry DD1 petals from the same area of the ombré roll. Cup the petals, colored side concave on the raspberry, and roll the bases around ¼" of hot glue while it cools into little plastic rods. Pull the petal tips over a hat pin to curve back slightly, then pull your fingernail up the back of each tip to gently straighten. Hot glue the bases to the flower, placing the tips up and down randomly. Add another 12 peach/beige DD1 petals if you are not using curled petals in the following steps.

2 Fully outstretch ombré crepe located between 5½" and 8" from the end of the roll. Using a wide, firm paintbrush, laminate some to fully outstretched peach/beige crepe and cut three bicolored DD2 petals, then cut four raspberry DD2 petals. Cut three DD2 petals from peach/beige crepe that has been stretched between your hands as far as you can without forcing, and note that all remaining peach/beige petals will be cut from crepe stretched in this manner. Tacky glue stem wire up the white side of two

raspberry and one peach/beige petal, extending 1" below each. Close the petals over the wire, reopen the centers, then roll into curled petal shapes. Cup the remaining petals, colored side in for the raspberry and peach side in for the bicolored petals. Roll the bases with hot glue and style the tips like the DD1 petals in step 1. Hot glue the petals randomly around the center, bending back to open outward ¾" to 1". Place curled petals closest to the center, and tilt the bicolored ones a bit to show both colors. Stack some petals right behind others and position petal tips high and low, avoiding perfectly staggered patterns. Add an additional 12 peach/beige DD2 petals if not using curled petals. Trim away excess bases and wires.

3 Fully outstretch ombré crepe located between 5" and 8¾" from the end of the roll. Use for four DD3 petals and laminate to fully outstretched peach/beige crepe for 12 bicolored DD3 petals. Cut 20 DD3 petals from peach/beige crepe stretched per step 2. Run stem wire up one peach/beige, the uncolored sides of the four raspberry, and the peach side of four bicolored petals. Close the petals over the wires and arch the bicolored petals backward, opening partway. Reopen the rest at the centers, then roll into curled petal shapes, some loose and some tighter. Cup the remaining petals, raspberry side out for the bicolored petals. Diagonally crease and curl about half of them per step 5 of the open-centered dahlia on page 160. Bend back the tips of the rest like the DD1 petals in step 1, folding a few to partly close with a crease up the back. Roll all the bases closed over ½" hot glue.

4 Follow step 2 for attaching DD3 petals irregularly around and down the flower, bending the unwired petal bases back and opening up between 1" and 2" from the inner petals, with most of the outer tips 3" from the center of the flower.

CONTINUED

5 Cut anywhere between 24 and 48 DD4 petals (depending on how full you want your flower) from peach/beige crepe stretched per step 2. Cup each petal, then do several of the following to groom them: pull top halves over a hat pin to curl back, run a fingernail up the backside to crease, then apply a little hot glue to the backside of the crease to reinforce it and the backward curve of the petal tip; run a thumbnail up the center of the face, causing the petal to close inward and the sides to become wavy; crease both sides of the face diagonally like step 5 of the open-center dahlia on page 160, then deeply pleat those crease lines by pulling the top half of the petal over a hat pin; or roll both top edges of the tip backward over a hat pin. Roll all the bases closed with ¾" to 1" hot glue.

Trim any petal bases, wire, and other bulk from the base of the flower. Place the DD4 petals around the flower with hot glue, with the tips reaching out to 3½" from the center of the flower. Begin to transition the petal bases to the stem, bending back less and sitting gradually straighter while moving down the flower and inward toward the stem. Cut away the excess bases from the inner petals, but keep the bases of the final layers of petals intact and apply the hot glue neatly at the bottom of the flower.

6 Monitor the face of the flower for a more-or-less even perimeter as you work, even if you leave gaps and place the petals in irregular patterns. Bottommost petals will sit more or less horizontally, and if the flower is very full they will start to point downward.

7 Wrap the stem tightly with two layers of light-green floral tape. Dab generously with crimson liquid concentrated watercolor and wipe up and down with an old kitchen towel to blend it into the stem.

For the double calyx, cut two 1½"-tall by 2½"-long strips of outstretched 180 gram #600/5 green-yellow ombré crepe paper from the center of the roll. Fold each strip over onto itself six times and cut a wide, round-topped triangle into each, leaving ¼" uncut at the bottom of the strips. Cup the uncolored side of each triangle, then hot glue one strip high around the base of the dahlia, evenly spaced. Secure the individual sepals to the underside of the flower with tacky glue, bending a few of the tips backward. Repeat with the second strip, staggered between the first. For the outer calyx layer, fold a piece of 1½"-tall by 3½"-long olive green doublette into six layers, place either the smaller DB-CALYX or the larger DH-CALYX template on top, and cut around, leaving a ⅛" strip uncut at the bottom. If a waxy finish is desired, coat both sides of the leaflets (not the bottom strip) with Mod Podge and let dry. Cup each leaflet and crease up the inside with your fingernail. Tacky glue the uncut bottom strip and ¼" up each leaflet on the cupped side, evenly spaced around the underside of the base of the flower (or the back of the bud, if making), overlapping the bottom strip as you go to shorten the length between each leaflet. Although five to eight leaflets are standard, I prefer to make six to eight for a fuller look.

When the glue has dried, bend the leaflets back sharply at the top of the glued-on portions, bending every other one farther back. Bend the stem just below the dahlia heads (and buds) down almost 90 degrees.

8 My favorite dahlias are the ones that are less dense, ones that look like they never developed into a full flower. I love making the twisted and curled petals, and the unexpected raspberry accents. The centers and a few surrounding petals can also be made from English Rose or Orchid single-ply crepe, which is not as durable for the curls, but matches the center color of these dahlias found in nature almost exactly.

open-centered dahlia

Tacky glue

60 gram #296 yellow
crepe paper

180 gram #568 brown
crepe paper

180 gram #581 orange
crepe paper

180 gram #558
lime green crepe paper

White doublette
crepe paper

180 gram #584 maroon
crepe paper

18-gauge brown paper-
wrapped stem wire

24-gauge white cloth-
covered stem wire

Lemon-yellow chalk

Blending brush

Dark-brown floral tape

Leaves (see page 198)

An open-centered dahlia is one where the center disc, or "the center," as I refer to it, is visible and easily pollinated. I love the look of these flowers. This specific one, with its white petals and dark foliage, is called the Swan Lake. It can be adapted to many other open-centered dahlias by replacing the white doublette petals with light yellow, light salmon, apricot, or red doublette crepes. Use the yellow-and-red candy-striped paper Pattern 3 on page 114 for the Patricia dahlia, a real stunner.

This tutorial includes a somewhat detailed brown and golden yellow center that attempts to mimic a mature dahlia center, and should receive the darker dahlia foliage shown on page 193. The centers can also be completely yellow, or a reddish brown, so feel free to replace the brown fringe with yellow or scarlet crepe, if you prefer. They can be used in the middle of the Dinnerplate Dahlia on page 153 as well, which look terrific with many swirly, curly petals dancing around the yellow stamens.

As always, skip the composite flower center and replace with plain fine fringe, if you'd rather.

1 Peel away ⅜" paper from the top of the brown stem wire and hook down. Cut two ¾"-tall by 8"-long strips of fine fringe, one from 60 gram #296 yellow crepe paper, the other from outstretched 180 gram #568 brown crepe paper. Adhere the bottoms of the two fringe strips together with tacky glue, the yellow strip staggered ¹⁄₁₆" below the top of the brown. Set aside a 2" segment for use in step 2. Apply glue to the bottom of the brown side, interlock with the hook, and wrap tightly, brown side in, with the top of fringe level. Spindle lightly after wrapping.

2 Cut eight 1"-tall by 3"-long strips of yellow crepe, and four of 180 gram #581 orange crepe paper. Laminate strips of yellow crepe to both sides of a strip of orange crepe using tacky glue. Create four twisted fringe strips by cutting ¾"-deep slits spaced ⅛" apart across each of the laminated strips, then twisting each ⅛"-wide piece onto itself as shown on page 87. Do one strip at a time, twisting the fringe while the paper is still moist from lamination for best results. Snip the tips with tiny scissors into subtle rounded points.

Glue and wrap one segment of twisted fringe ⅛" up from the inner fringe. Bend the tips slightly inward. Add the remaining 2" of brown-and-yellow fine fringe from step 1, brown side in, aligning the top with the twisted fringe.

3 Wrap a second segment of twisted fringe around the center, top aligned with the first segment, tips bent inward slightly, followed by a third segment of twisted fringe, tips straight but aligned with the first two, stretching slightly as you go.

4 Bend the tips of the final 3" segment of twisted fringe 30 degrees. With the tips bending outward from the center, apply glue to the bottom and up the back of each twisted spike to where it bends. Wrap, stretching lightly, ⅛" below the top of the

previous segments. Press lightly to adhere, and bend any stray tips back out after glue has set.

5 Two at a time, cut 16 petals from white doublette using template OD1, setting one aside for step 7. Following the template guidelines, pull a deep diagonal crease into the left side of each petal using your right thumbnail, and vice versa, creating a tall, slightly open triangle shape in the center. Repeat several times to imprint.

6 Stretch the center of each triangle with your thumbnail moving from base to tip, then go over the creases a final time to reinforce. Apply tacky glue at the bottom ¼" of each petal, fold over the left side and then the right, and squeeze to secure, keeping the face of each petal open. Rub lemon-yellow chalk into the bottom center of each petal with a blending brush. Roll the tops of the petals on each side back at an angle with a hat pin, then roll the sides back gently. Fold and stretch a few petals to look irregular, if desired.

7 To create unfurling petals near the center, cut two OD4 petals from white doublette crepe and cup the centers. Cut pieces of white stem wire 1" taller than each petal and glue up the center of their inside faces. Pinch the petal bases and tips, keeping the petal midsections more open. Repeat with the larger OD1 petal reserved from step 5, pinching the top closed and folding the bottom open.

8 Finely fringe a ¾"-tall by 3"-long strip of yellow crepe and wrap around ⅛" down from the center one time without overlapping the ends. Bend each wired petal back 90 degrees at its base, then curl them inward, giving each its own appearance of unfurling. Glue the three petals randomly about the center, just below the bends in the twisted fringe spikes. Curl the petal edges over a hat pin this way and that for a natural look. Trim away excess white wire.

CONTINUED

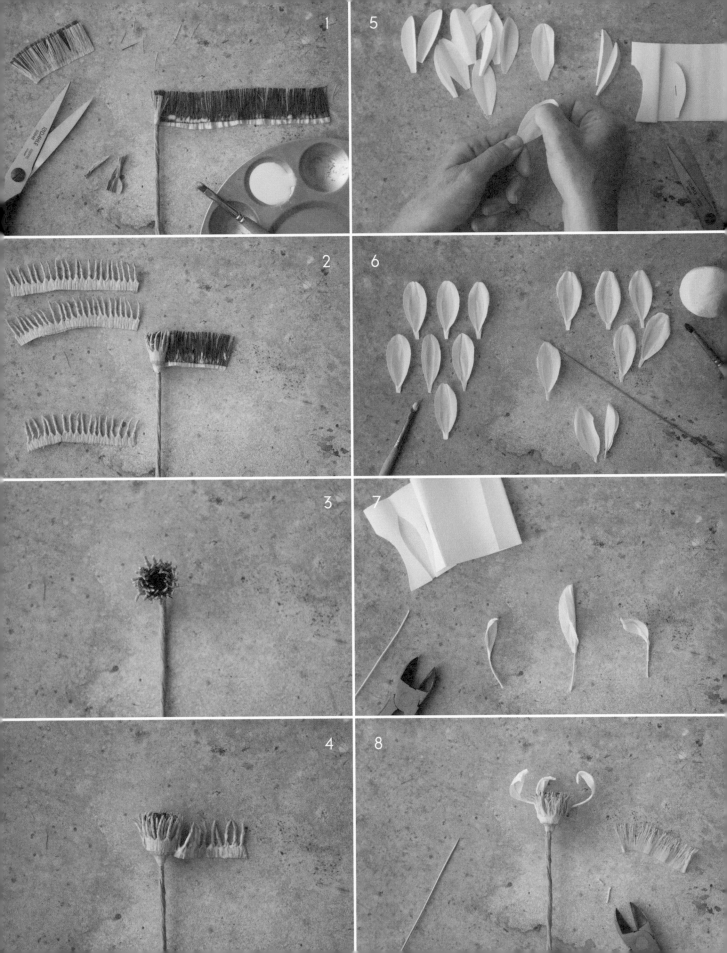

9 Bend the bottom of each of the 15 creased OD1 petals back ¼". Dip the bent bottoms into tacky glue and attach around the flower, filling in as shown. Remember which way is up on your flower if you would like to follow the petal layouts in the photographs. Most petals should be attached without any twisting in their faces, just shy of ⅛" below the center of the flower. The tips of the petals should sit between ½" and ¾" above the top of the center.

10 Use any petals that did not fit in the first row to fill in gaps below, holding snugly to the upper row.

11 Cut 12 OD2 petals two at a time from white doublette. Cup each petal, then crease diagonally along each side following the petal template, leaving a small opening between the two creases at the top of the petals. Stretch the center of each triangle with your thumbnail moving from base to tip, then go over the creases a final time to reinforce. One at a time, fold each side of the petal over at its crease. Hold the crease closed while cupping the side of the petal at its back, then repeat at the other side. This helps give the petal faces more depth and dimension.

12 Gather the bottom ¼" of each petal by folding each side of the base in on itself aligned with the creases on each side. Pinch the bases together, keeping the petal faces open. Curl the top edges and some of the sides back lightly over a hat pin at a small downward angle, then reinforce the creases at the top of the petals by wiping a very small amount of tacky glue with the hat pin into the top ¼" of the creases. Slide the hat pin out, adhering the creases ever-so-slightly, which will accentuate them and keep them crisp. Trim away any petal edges that may have become too wide, and brush yellow chalk into the bottoms of the petals.

13 Glue a ¾"-tall strip of outstretched 180 gram #558 lime green crepe paper just below the OD1 petals. Bend the OD2 petal bases back just a hair over ¼", dip the bent ends in tacky glue, and attach tight to the bottom of the first row of petals. The petals will point slightly downward naturally.

14 Stagger some of the petals just a little, while centering others fully between the petals of the first row. Find balance between nesting some petals and staggering others. Squeeze the base tightly several times while adding the petals.

15 Cut 26 OD3 petals two at a time from white doublette. How many you will need is a little up to chance, but it is usually in the 22 to 26 range. Style, groom, and gather the petals per steps 11 and 12, then bend back the bases just a hair over ¼" and attach just below the second petal row. Stagger and center the petals in different ways around the flower. The petals will be angled down, but try not to let them hang so far down that they droop too much.

16 Eyeball the face of the flower to see where it needs to be filled out. Squeeze the base tightly several times as you go to compact it. These dahlias can be found with two or more rows of petals, so feel free to vary the number of petals from flower to flower. Wrap the stem in dark-brown floral tape, or wrap first with outstretched strips of 180 gram #584 maroon crepe paper before the dark-brown floral tape to give it a bit of a reddish-purple glow. Calyx information can be found in the Dinnerplate Dahlia tutorial on page 153. Dark dahlia leaves are extra fun to make. Consider adding some to your dahlia stem for a unique touch.

double bomb peony

Tacky glue

Hot glue

180 gram #600/4
rose ombré crepe paper

180 gram #580
red orange crepe paper
(optional)

180 gram #576/9
candy corn ombré crepe
paper (optional)

180 gram #564
blue green crepe paper

Light-green floral tape

18-gauge brown paper-
wrapped stem wire

Black coffee (optional)

Leaves (see page 195)

Given my wide study of peonies, for both my large-scale fine art pieces and my truer-to-scale smaller versions, it can sometimes take an explosive confection of a peony like the double bomb to get my attention. Their oversize globular forms are both elegant and ridiculous, as are their funny names, like Mister Ed and Many Happy Returns. In my opinion, some types of peonies do not translate well in paper, but I believe these do.

Despite appearances, double bomb peonies are one of the fastest and easiest flowers in this book, if you work smart. The speed comes from using your fingertips to apply the glue to crimp the bases of the petaloids, and then taking advantage of that tackiness to apply them to the flower in rapid succession, without stopping to paint glue on each with a brush. It will also simplify things if you use the templates as general shape and size guides rather than cutting around them. You can vary petal amounts for fuller or looser globes. My take on the globular flower form falls somewhere between party decoration and serious botanical specimen, with some guidance on how to adapt for a flower that has begun to fall open. These are stunners in hot and bright corals, magentas and reds, pastels, and different combinations of colors as well.

1 Finely fringe and spindle an outstretched ½"-tall by 1¾"-long piece of the lightest crepe paper from a 180 gram #600/4 rose ombré roll, or use outstretched #580 red orange and #576/9 candy corn orange ombré crepe together for more pop. Spiral the fringe down compactly around the top of the stem wire, pinching at the base to create a tuft. For a falling-open bloom, skip to step 4. For a full double bomb, cut an assortment of DB1 to DB5 petals from outstretched rose ombré crepe, making sure the tips are always lighter than the bases. Cut twelve from the lighter section located between 6" and 8½" from the end of the roll, 64 from the medium section located between 4" and 6½" from the end, and eight from the darker section located between ½" and 3" from the end.

2 Starting with the twelve lightest-colored petals, crimp eight at a time (maximum) to keep the glue at a good tackiness for attaching them to the flower. Swipe your finger lightly through tacky glue, wipe the glue in a thin layer down the back bottom 1" of each petal, and crimp the base. Make an upward-facing crease in most type DB1 and DB5 petals, and cup on each side of the crease by pulling between your thumb and forefinger. Leave a few DB1 and DB5 petals flat, but a majority of them should be creased to add volume or to fill in between other petals. Petal types DB2 to DB4 should be stretched gently convex or concave, or creased upward from bottom to top with a bit of a backward bend. Press the bottom ¾" of each of these 12 petals to the stem just below the fringed center while the glue is still tacky, petals standing upright.

3 Repeat step 2 with 24 of the 64 medium-hued petals, eight at a time, aligning their bottoms at the stem. Attach them radially, emanating from the center and not twisting. Avoid striation by layering upward creased petals behind flatter petals, and vice versa, never nesting them. The rounded bloom should form naturally, but adjust as needed. Repeat step 2 with the eight darkest petals, which will lay almost horizontally and attach evenly around the flower. Pinch the base together tightly to round the form, then skip to step 5.

4 For a more open-centered peony, cut an assortment of 44 DB6 to DB10 petals in the color of your choice. Bend 16 of these backward at the base, grooming per step 2 with creases facing up. Attach just below the fringed center, with the petal tips 1" up from the center. Apply the remaining 28 petals per step 3, angling the bottom petals slightly downward. Make a stain made from 180 gram #564 blue green crepe paper soaked in water and dab around the base of the fringe center, then skip to step 6..

5 Attach the remaining 40 medium-hued petals to the globular form per step 3. Their tips should protrude out slightly from the darker petals above, with the bottommost petals angled slightly downward. Handle by their tips while placing if bases get too sticky. Squeeze the base together again tightly.

6 For the six guard petals, cut two 3¾"-tall by 3½"-long strips of crepe from the lightest part of the rose ombré roll, outstretching each to 6" long. Fold each strip into three layers, and cup all three layers at once, creating a wide, circular bowl at one end of both folded strips. Cut around the circular indentation to create tapered, spoon-shaped petals with 2"-diameter bowls. Gather the bottoms with tacky glue and bend back 1". Guard petals can also be made with unstretched 5" lengths of 60 gram crepe, or 5" lengths of 100 gram crepe outstretched to 7".

7 Space the six petals equally around the base of the flower with hot glue at the bend in each petal. Weather the petal edges with a few jagged cuts and dabs of black coffee if desired. Cut away excess paper at the base, then wrap the stems with light-green floral tape. For leaf placement and calyx details, see the Faded Coral Charm Peony on page 169.

8 Change it up by using 180 gram #580 red orange petaloids with 60 gram #319 deep red guard petals or plain or bleach-dipped 180 gram #601 coral crepe all over. Try adding a second row of six guard petals staggered below the first if you'd like. Wrap the stems in outstretched blue green crepe for an interesting contrast.

faded coral charm peony

Tacky glue

Hot glue

100 gram green tea
crepe paper

Olive green doublette
crepe paper

Black coffee

Red ink or crimson
liquid watercolor

18-gauge brown paper-
wrapped stem wire

Leaves (see page 195)

FADED CORAL CHARM

180 gram #567 light brown
crepe paper

100 gram ivory crepe paper

100 gram gold crepe paper

**BRIGHTER FADED
CORAL CHARM**

180 gram #576 deep yellow
crepe paper

100 gram white crepe paper

180 gram #566 pale green
crepe paper

Pink chalk or unscented
pink-mauve blush

Blending brush

Light-green floral tape

The ever-popular Coral Charm peony is a luscious, layered specimen, whose color is hard to replicate. The pains one could go through to re-create that perfect, glowing coral pink are too great, especially to someone like me, who likes to let the form of the flower do much of the talking.

Lucky for me, the lifespan of a cut Coral Charm peony is short. The blooms lose steam quickly, fading from bright pink to pale beige to white in just a matter of days. This faded Coral Charm catches them in their open form during the last days before the petals fall off in clumps.

As is characteristic of the form of this peony, there are lots of stacked petals. One of the best ways to keep these stacks looking natural on the flower is to cut and cup several petals at a time and keep them in those stacks. This ensures they will have similar shape and contour to one another and will look as if they've been nested in each other before the flower fell open. I've also included variations for a slightly brighter, whiter Coral Charm. You can experiment with blending pink chalk or unscented pink-mauve blush into the petals, ever so faintly, here and there, or try using 100 gram peach/beige crepe for more colorful petals. To color your petals for a Pink Spinner, the candy-striped version of this peony, see Pattern 6 on page 114. Fold and cup the petal paper per step 4, then cut out large and small petals using PS-Large and PS-Small.

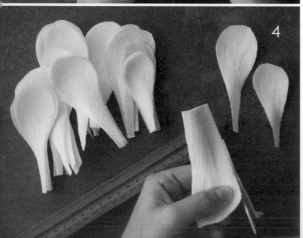

1 Create three laminated fringe strips, each from a 1⅞"-tall by 4"-long strip of 180 gram #567 light brown crepe paper tacky glued between similarly sized strips of outstretched 100 gram ivory crepe on one side and outstretched 100 gram gold crepe on the other, with the brown strip ⅛" above the outer strips. Trim each strip to 1½" tall by 4" long. Finely fringe along the light brown edge, leaving ⁵⁄₁₆" uncut at the bottom.

For brighter stamens, replace the light brown center strip with 180 gram #576 deep yellow crepe and sandwich between two strips of outstretched 100 gram white crepe.

Note: Be sure to complete step 2 while the fringe strips are still malleable, but wait 5 to 10 minutes before spindling the fringe to prevent it from sticking together.

2 For the carpels at the center of the peony, bend the top of a stem wire into a tight ½"-tall M shape. Bend a 1" segment of the same wire in half to make an upside down U, then hot glue it tightly to the M for three visible carpels. For a brighter center, cover the top of the stem wire and each end of two 2"-long stem wire segments with light-green floral tape, then cover all five ends with outstretched 180 gram #566 pale green crepe paper. Bend the 2" segments into U shapes, and hot glue together at the top of the stem wire to create a tight ring of five carpels. Use the blending brush to dust the tops lightly with blush or pink chalk.

Create three stamen segments by folding the three fringe strips onto themselves in Z shapes, stepping down ¹⁄₁₆" after each fold in the Z, with the white fringe facing up at the lowest part. Gather each segment tightly together at its base, sealing between the folds with tacky glue, then spindle the fringe tightly and rub your fingers through vigorously to rough it up. Splay the stamen pieces out from side to side and front to back, creating wide, fuzzy wedges that will each fill one-third of the way around the carpels. Attach with hot glue at the base of each wedge, the tips ½" up from the carpels.

3 Cut eight 4"-tall by 5"-long strips of 100 gram ivory crepe for the faded peony, or 100 gram white crepe for a brighter one. Fold each strip in half, then in half again, then firmly stretch and cup all four layers at once, creating a wide, circular bowl at the end of each folded segment. Repeat with two 3"-tall by 4"-long strips of the same color paper.

4 Cut around the circular indentation through the four layers of crepe on each folded segment, creating 32 tapered spoon-shaped petals with 1⅜"-diameter bowls from the larger segments, and eight tapered spoon-shaped petals with 1⅛"-diameter bowls from the smaller ones. Keep the petals nested in their stacks of four.

5 Crumple one smaller and four larger petal stacks by gathering and crushing the edge of the bowls at each side, then mashing the tops a bit with your fingers.

6 Pleat the bases of the crumpled petals onto themselves with tacky glue, gathering the bottom ¾" of the smaller petals and the bottom 1" of the larger petals. Cut a mitten shape into one of the small and three of the larger petals. Pinch the backsides of two of the larger petals together with a bit of glue for more petal variation.

7 Bend the small petal bases back ¾" and the larger petal bases back 1", keeping petals in their respective stacks. Attach the four crumpled, smaller petals with hot glue on each face right above the bend, pressing upward to adhere to the underside of the stamens. Locate these petals at 10, 12, 2, and 5 o'clock as shown. Remember where 12 o'clock is on your flower if you would like to follow the petal layouts in the photographs. Nest two larger crumpled petals behind the petals at the 10 and 2 positions, and add a third at 7 o'clock.

8 Lift three petals off each of the three remaining stacks of larger crumpled petals and hot glue the bases and bottom faces of each set together. Use hot glue to attach the sets to the underside of the stamens, placing

CONTINUED

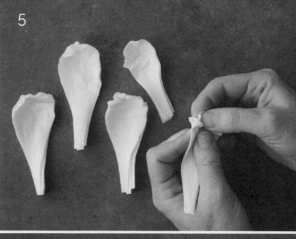

one set behind the smaller petal at 12, one at about 4, and one at 8 o'clock. Separate the petals a bit, coax upward slightly, and trim away the loose petal bases.

9 Gather the bases of all the smooth petals per step 6, and bend the bases back per step 7. Following hot glue petal attachment details from previous steps, attach four large smooth petals tipped sideways at slight angles and staggered behind existing nested petals at the 1, 4, 10, and 12 o'clock positions. Additionally, add a set of two large crumpled petals nested in a smooth large petal at 8:30 to 9, and another around 6 o'clock. Cut away loose bases.

10 Slide the remaining four small, smooth petals in around the flower to fill closer to the center. Attach a few of these pointing more upward, as if hanging on before falling open. Use larger smooth petals nested in sets of two or by themselves to fill around the rest of the peony, with the bottommost petals angled down slightly. Bend the bases back farther up the petals if the petals start to look too long.

11 Cut away the loose petal bases and use wire cutters to carefully snip away any excess glue and paper buildup that will come away without damaging your flower. Tacky glue a strip of 100 gram green tea crepe paper with a ripped top edge around the remaining base. Create opened peony bud cover pieces by laminating 2"-tall layers of green tea paper together. Cup the laminated paper deeply and cut different cupped sepals from it using BUD COVER1 to 3 templates. Make a quick stain using 1 tablespoon black coffee and 1 drop red ink or crimson liquid concentrated watercolor. Brush the stain lightly on the base of the flower and each side of the covers. Let dry.

12 Place a combination of two or three small peony leaves and a few bud cover pieces strategically around the base with hot glue. Tacky glue ¾"-tall by ¼"-wide pointed sepal bits cut from paper to match your stem wrap around the very bottom of the base if you need more help transitioning, but these are not required. Peony stems are often light-green and look great with darker leaves.

ranunculus

Tacky glue

Hot glue

160 gram golden yellow
crepe paper, stretched as
far as you can between
your hands without
forcing, and colored per
Pattern 7 on page 114

180 gram moss green
crepe paper

180 gram #562 dusty
green crepe paper
(optional)

100 gram scarlet crepe
paper (optional)

160 gram light salmon
crepe paper (optional)

Loosely pressed golden
metallic eyeshadow

Blending brush

Light-green floral tape

18-gauge brown paper-
wrapped stem wire

Mod Podge (optional)

Pink chalk dust (optional)

Leaves (see page 199)

A beautiful striated ranunculus closes this chapter on a high note. It's something no paper flower book should be without. If the sky was the limit, I would also include small, tightly layered ranunculuses, curly swirly Charlotte ranunculuses, open ranunculuses with exposed stamens, and maybe one on the decline, resembling a stack of paper that is about to fall over. But for now, my favorite ranunculus form will have to do: a bloom that is closed in the center and irregularly layered, with petal tips that are rounded and squarish at the same time. The version shown on the following pages here uses paper treated to be a "Café Caramel" color, but choose whichever color you'd like. You can find ranunculus growing in shades of pink, red, orange, yellow, purple, and white. If using 160 or 180 gram crepe, the paper should be stretched as far as you can between your hands without forcing, but 100 gram crepe can remain unstretched.

I stopped teaching paper ranunculus workshops after my first few attempts, because if my students didn't catch all the little details along the way, we ended up with a room full of (still beautiful) roses instead of ranunculuses. So please trust my methods here and pay close attention. There are clock-face numbers for petal placement that may not make sense at first, but they are quite intentional. If you do get lost, just start again wherever you are on the flower. Holding each petal to the flower to test how it will sit before you attach it can be very helpful. This is a wonderful specimen, one that makes me very happy. It's well worth the work!

1 Prepare 7' of 2"-tall paper strips from the stretched and colored 160 gram golden yellow crepe paper. Hook the top of the stem wire down ¼" and wrap floral tape tightly around into a ⅞"-diameter ball. Tacky glue a scrap of petal paper to the top of the ball. Cut 32 R1, 12 R2, 10 R3, 10 R4, and 22 R5 petals with their tops along the black edge of the colored paper. Cup 12 R1 petals with their painted sides out and use a blending brush to blend in golden metallic eyeshadow (throughout this tutorial, always apply the eyeshadow to the painted side of the petal ⅛" below the top edge). Attach with tacky glue at their concave bellies at 12 and 6 o'clock, their top edges ¹⁄₁₆" apart, up ¹⁄₁₆" from the top of the ball. Add two petals one behind the other at 1 o'clock, then one at 5 o'clock just above the center ones. Locate the next three up a hair at 2:30, 3 o'clock, and 4:30. Place a petal just above the center ones at 9 o'clock, then a hair above that at 11, 10, and 9 o'clock.

2 Use hot glue to attach the petals in the remainder of the steps, applying it higher on the petals when closing them inward and lower on the petals when required to open a bit. Of the remaining 20 R1 petals, cup half painted side out and half painted side in, lightly stretching the top edge of each to remove some of the curve. Remember to add eyeshadow to the painted side of each one. Place petals with painted sides out a hair higher than the ones from step 1 at 11, 1, 2, and 3 o'clock, then 11 and 12 o'clock and 12:30, closing inward. Place one at 9 o'clock painted side in, gluing at its base so it will tilt slightly open. Place the final three painted-side-out petals at 7 and 5 o'clock, then 4:30. The remaining nine painted-side-in petals should sit slightly higher than the previous petals, with a corner slightly curled back or one or both sides rolled back.

They should also sit more vertically, with the final three opening slightly more dramatically. Place them in order at 5:30, 3 o'clock, and 1 o'clock, 1:30, 5:30, 6 o'clock, 7:30, 9 o'clock, and 7 o'clock. Trim away excess paper bulk at the bottom of the flower.

3 All remaining petals should be attached with their painted sides in. Very lightly stretch the backsides at the tops of the 12 R2 petals to flatten and bend backward slightly, then cup low on their front faces. Very lightly ripple the top edges of a few with your thumbnail. Gather their bottoms with tacky glue and dust with golden eyeshadow. Attach with hot glue near their bases, their tips about ⅛" above the previous petals at 7 o'clock, 5:30, staggered just a hair off of 5:30, 4:30, 4 and 3 o'clock, 1:30, 1 o'clock, 12:30, 11 o'clock, 10:30, and 10 o'clock. The outer R2 petals should hug lower on the flower and open up at the tips, while the inner ones can sit a little more vertically with edges just starting to roll back. The highest petals of the flower should land at about ½" above the center ball.

4 Style the 10 R3 petals like the R2 petals, bending their top portions back slightly more and rolling one or both side edges back on a few. Gather the bottom ⅜" of each with tacky glue and bend back, dust with eyeshadow, then apply hot glue just above the bends and attach at 9 o'clock, 8:30, 6:30, 2:30, 3:30, 1:30, 12:30, 10 and 11 o'clock, and 4:30. The petals around the lower half of the clock face should be similar in height to the ones in step 3, while the petals starting to form the next layer out should fall open with their tips ⅛" to ¼" down and out from the inner petals. Snip off the petal bases after attaching.

CONTINUED

5 Trim away the excess bulk at the base of the flower again. The remaining petals should be spaced down the flower a little bit farther apart to start to conceal the bulk, eventually blending back in toward the stem for a smooth transition, with the ends of the final petal bases from step 6 touching the stem.

Stretch the center of the top edges at the backside of the 10 R4 petals, then trim just a little off the top of each to create a slightly jagged, squared-off edge. Roll one or both side edges back on a few petals, gather the bottom ⅜" of each with tacky glue, and bend back. Dust each with eyeshadow and attach with hot glue at the bend at 3 o'clock, 1:30, 1 and 5 o'clock, extending out slightly farther at 7:30, 12:30, 1:30, 5 o'clock, 5:30, and 6 o'clock. These petals should fall open with their tips ⅛" or so down and out from the petals before them. Observe the face of the flower as you work to keep it balanced. Use petals with curled-back side edges to fill in vertically at odd gaps. Set the petals gradually lower on the flower without creating unnaturally large gaps between the layers. Snip away the unglued base of each petal after attaching.

6 Lightly stretch the top edges of the 22 R5 petals, keeping them flat. Gather the bottom ⅜" of each with tacky glue. Dust with eyeshadow and roll one or both side edges back on about half of them with a little stretch to add volume. Apply hot glue between ¼" and ½" above the bottom of each petal and place at 4 and 3 o'clock, then 2:30, 3:30, 5:30, 9 o'clock, 8 and 10 o'clock, 10:30, 11 o'clock, 12:30, and 12 o'clock. Finish with petals at 10:30, 1 o'clock, 6:30, 7:30, 3 and 9 o'clock, 9:30, 8 and 7 o'clock, and 7:30, adjusting to fill in at your discretion. Remember to move down the flower enough and start to attach petals to the flower's underside to achieve that smooth transition at the bottom. Trim the

bases off of the inner R5 petals, but glue the bottom ones down to neatly cover the underside of the flower with the bases touching the stem. The petals should curve out and open with their tips extending out just slightly farther than the ones above them.

I prefer a less full, more uneven flower, so I like to roughly curl and tuck many petal edges back deeply with my fingers to open up spaces between them and make the whole flower look a little messier. Petals that seem too long can be crushed in or rolled back to shorten, or you can carefully trim them. Wrap the stem with outstretched 180 gram moss green crepe paper.

7 This flower looks great without its sepals, but if you'd like to add some, laminate ten 1¼"-long pieces of light-green floral tape to outstretched 180 gram dusty green crepe paper right next to each other. Align the centerline of template R6 along the joint between two pieces of tape and cut a sepal. Repeat another four times, then cup the tape side of each by running your fingernail radially outward from its middle a dozen or so times, creating a bit of texture on the outer paper side. Gather the bottom third of each and attach evenly around the base of the flower at the stem with tacky glue, then wrap additional outstretched moss green crepe to cover the bases.

8 My other favorite ranunculus colors include plain, unstretched 100 gram scarlet crepe and 160 gram light salmon crepe, stretched as instructed in the materials list, with a mixture of Mod Podge and pink chalk dust brushed quickly into the bottom half of each petal and dusted with golden eyeshadow. The Mod Podge can replace the tacky glue for gathering petal bases, if used. Experiment with setting the outer petals lower or higher to achieve different ranunculus profiles and forms.

5

6

7

8

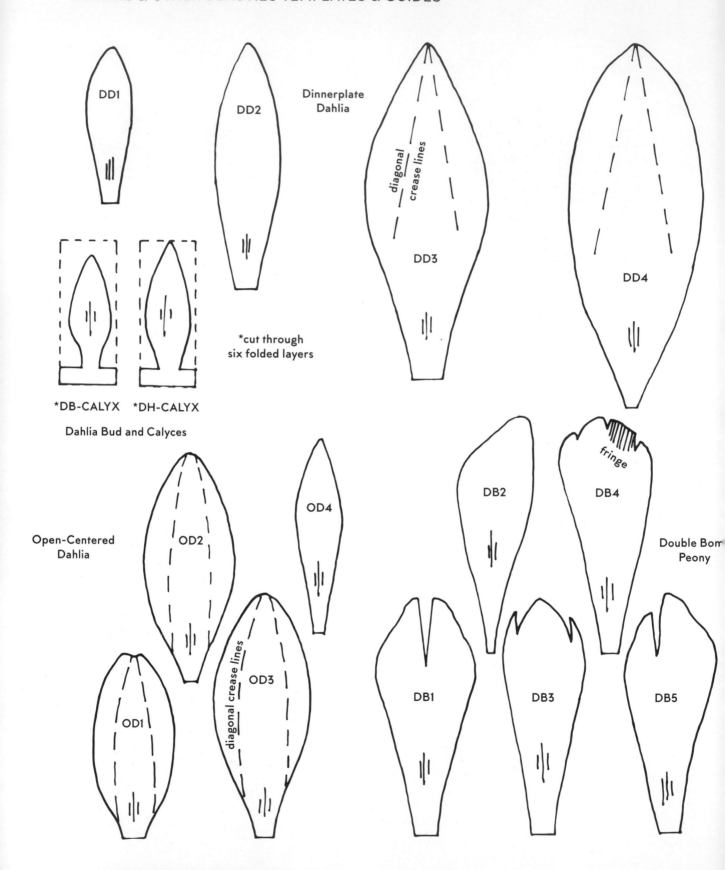

DD1

DD2

Dinnerplate Dahlia

diagonal crease lines

DD3

DD4

*DB-CALYX   *DH-CALYX

Dahlia Bud and Calyces

*cut through
six folded layers

OD2

OD4

Open-Centered
Dahlia

DB2

DB4

fringe

Double Bom
Peony

OD1

diagonal crease lines   OD3

DB1

DB3

DB5

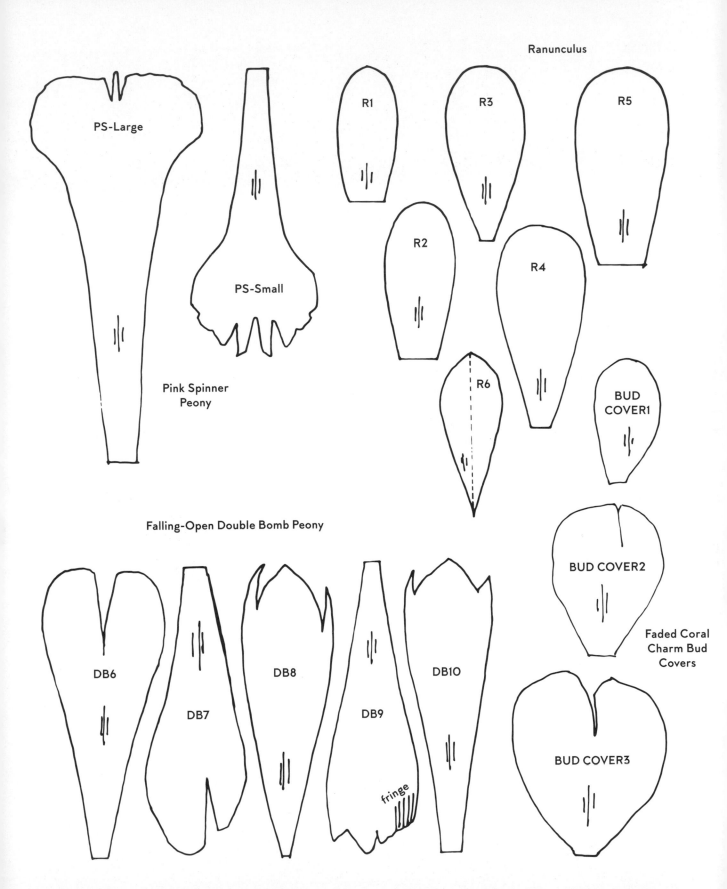

Ranunculus

PS-Large

PS-Small

Pink Spinner
Peony

R1

R3

R5

R2

R4

R6

BUD
COVER1

Falling-Open Double Bomb Peony

BUD COVER2

Faded Coral
Charm Bud
Covers

DB6

DB7

DB8

DB9

DB10

fringe

BUD COVER3

CHAPTER 3

leaves, stems & buds

185

leaf construction

In general, most paper leaves are made from two leaf blades, or sides, adhered together with a thin line of tacky glue along their straight inner edges, similar to the bougainvillea bracts at the start of this book. The grain of the paper on the templates is oriented at angles upward and outward from the leaf centers to mimic the veins. When leaf sides are too small or cumbersome to cut out easily, like carnation and dahlia leaves, the full leaf can be cut out at once by aligning the template's center rib line along the intersection of two larger pieces of crepe paper that are already glued together with the grain pointed upward and outward. Paper leaves are often groomed to bend and wave depending on the type, and, in most cases, thin floral wire is set in a thin line of tacky glue along the back or front of the leaves or hidden within the overlap between the two blades.

Templates and instructions for leaf assemblies by flower type are covered at the end of this chapter, in the order they appear in the book. Basic rose leaves are included, and discussed in detail on page 188, along with other rose stem components. Making leaf templates is as simple as tracing a leaf, and I encourage you to do your own field studies. Observing branch configurations in nature is much easier than trying to learn them from a book.

What might be the most botanically accurate may not always be the easiest on the eyes when it comes to green crepe paper. In nature, many flower stems turn from brighter to darker as they age, so unless your leaf requires a very distinctive color, like the glaucous gray-blue-green of a certain poppy leaf, use a little artistic license and select the greens that look best to you. Both 100 gram moss green and olive green doublette crepe can be used for a host of different leaves, and I enjoy using 180 gram green-yellow ombré paper for gradual color change across several leaves on the same stem.

ADDITIONAL LEAF CONSTRUCTION TIPS

- While the glue holding two leaf sides is setting up, press the glued edges together between your thumb and forefinger several times to ensure a tight, natural intersection of the two blades.

- Templates can be sized up and down as desired to achieve different sizes of the same type of leaf. The same template can be used for both sides of a symmetrical leaf, just be sure to orient the paper grain properly on each leaf blade. For more irregular leaves, templates with slightly different profiles are provided for each side to create an asymmetrical leaf when joined together. Trim leaf tips to even points with tiny scissors when needed after joining the two sides.

- Many flower stems are finished by wrapping them with floral tape, ⅛"- to ¼"-tall strips of outstretched crepe with a thin layer of tacky glue, or layers of both, and can be built up in thickness with either if desired. Leaf wires are attached to flower stems underneath the wrapping. The length of a wire on a leaf depends on leaf spacing and desired flower stem or branch thickness. Always be mindful of how much bulk you are adding to the flower stem when you attach the leaves. The rose leaves photo on page 189 gives an example of how to layer leaf stems properly.

- Red ink or watercolor, coffee, chalk, bleach, Mod Podge, and plain water can all be used on leaves to give them a variety of interesting details. Use techniques discussed in "Imperfections & Wilt—Dead Paper Flowers" on page 148 to create aged and dried leaves using the templates in this chapter.

rose leaves, stems, buds & more

These little details can help refine your work and add interest to your already beautiful paper roses. Experiment with shapes, shades, and, of course, imperfections.

ROSE LEAVES

The rose "leaves" referred to in this book (see page 195) are actually "leaflets," parts of a composite leaf typically made up of three, five, or seven leaflets. The main largest leaf is located at the top, followed by pairs of leaflets descending in size below. Attach the leaflets by bending their stem wires 1/16" to 1/8" below their bottoms and binding with floral tape or crepe strips in opposing pairs to the face of the main stem. Space the pairs 5/8" to 3/4" apart without overlapping the leaves. Clip each leaflet stem where the next pair is to be placed to keep the center stem (petiole) thin. Leave the center stem longer for attachment to the flower stem. Cut one green STPL stipule, then cup, curl the tips back, and attach behind the petiole where it meets the flower stem.

Cover the center stem and short leaflet stems (petiolules) by wrapping with floral tape or outstretched strips of green or maroon crepe, or brown crepe brushed with crimson liquid watercolor. Soften the transition at maroon petiolules by wetting the bottoms of the leaflets and dabbing with a touch of crimson.

ROSE CALYCES

Fold a strip of 1¾"-tall by 2"-long olive green doublette or outstretched green crepe into five layers and cut a point using CLX1 on page 81. Spindle, then cup each sepal. Bend back at the base and glue to the underside of the rose around the stem with the concave side facing out. Leave them longer or trim shorter if you'd like. For a neater look, use five floral-tape-and-paper sepals (see "Rose Buds"), bending the sepals downward after the glue has set.

ROSE BUDS

Loop a stem wire 3/8" from its end and wrap tightly with floral tape into a bud shape following guides RB1 to 3. Cut four rose petals using the Hybrid Tea Rose petal template HR1 on page 80. Cup the petals deeply, curl the upper edges, then stagger and spiral them around the bud base covering it. Laminate five strips of light-green floral tape to a piece of outstretched 180 gram #562 dusty green or 100 gram moss green crepe in the direction of the grain and cut five SPL sepal pieces when dry. Run a fingernail up the paper side of each several times to cup and crease them. Brush a mixture of pink chalk dust and Mod Podge onto the tape sides. Glue the sepal bases around the bottom of the bud, spaced evenly. Let set, then wrap a thin strip of olive green doublette below the sepals into a tapered ¼"-tall by 3/16"-wide bud base. Coat with the chalk/Mod Podge mixture. Open the sepals partially, with pinched tips pointing outward.

FALLEN ROSES

Make the center stamen cluster from the Iceberg Floribunda Rose tutorial step 1 on page 64, then wrap with 1¼" of light-brown stamen per step 6 of the same tutorial. For more wilt, try some stamens with dark-brown anthers and white filaments as well. Create petals with an aged or dried appearance using suggestions in "Imperfections & Wilt—Dead Paper Flowers" on page 148, or use petals made of doublette crepe brushed with black coffee for a wonderfully weathered effect. Tacky glue the base of one wilted petal down 5/16" from the stamen tips, then space five floral tape and crepe sepals (see "Rose Buds") evenly just below the petal. Let the glue set, then wrap thin strips of olive green doublette just below the sepals into a 5/16"-diameter spherical ovary and coat with Mod Podge. Bend the sepals downward toward the stem.

ROSE LEAVES

ROSE BUDS

ROSE CALYCES

FALLEN ROSES

dahlia bud

Create a ¾"-diameter by ½"-deep rounded, dislike bud with floral tape wrapped around a ¼" hook at the top of a wire matching your dahlia stem. Cut a DB-CALYX strip (page 180) from outstretched light yellow-green crepe folded onto itself six times, then glue five or six sepals around the base and over the bud. Gather at the face and trim away excess. Coat with Mod Podge, then tint the rounded portion of the face with pink chalk. Cut an olive green DB-CALYX and see step 7 on page 157 for attachment.

dandelion seed head & stem

For a dandelion seed head, finely fringe a ¾"-tall by 6"-long and a ⅜" by 24"-long strip of outstretched tea-stained 180 gram #600 white crepe paper. Interlock the 6" strip with the hook of an already prepared dandelion stem and wrap around with tacky glue, keeping level. Repeat with the longer strip, aligning the bottoms, then fluff the top with your finger. Cut 12 equally spaced ½"-deep pointed sepals in a 1⅛"-tall by 1¾"-long strip of olive green doublette and wrap around the bud just below the top of the fringe, applying tacky glue to the inner faces up to ¼" below the sepal tips. Pleat the base of one sepal over the next to fit them evenly around the bud, then smooth into a vase-like form. See step 8 on page 121 for the lower rows of bracts.

For a dandelion stem, taper the top 3" of an 18-gauge brown paper-wrapped wire. Create a ¼" bare hook at the top, then wrap the wire in the opposite direction as the twisting brown paper, first with thin, tacky glue strips of olive doublette, then with light-green floral tape. Rub the stem with yellow chalk and polish vigorously with an old kitchen towel to shine.

magnolia branches

Thicken an 18-gauge brown paper-wrapped stem wire by wrapping with five layers of floral tape. Taper the top ¾" before wrapping the stem with ¼" strips of outstretched 180 moss green crepe. Round the tip and bend the tapered top ¾" 30 degrees. For a forked branch, wrap another 18-gauge wire tightly with tape three times before covering with crepe to use for the thinner offshoot.

Tacky glue small, irregular patches of olive green doublette crepe along the branch, letting intermittent pops of the bright moss green paper show through. Let each sit 30 seconds before peeling off to reveal natural-looking residue. If the residue doesn't adhere, press the paper back down and scrape it with your fingernail to thin the paper for a similar effect. Alternatively, you can wrap the entire branch with strips of outstretched 180 gram #567 light brown crepe, which is the perfect color for an aging magnolia branch, but doesn't leave residue easily.

Prepare magnolia leaves per page 199 in assorted sizes. Bend the very end of the light-brown portion of each leaf stem into a 90-degree elbow, bend the unwrapped portion of the wire back down 90 degrees, then attach by wrapping the unfinished wire and branch together with paper to match the color in that area. Locate three or four smallish leaves facing each other starting at the base of the tapered tip, staggering them around and down ⅜" from each other. Stagger medium-size leaves down 1" to 2", oriented to face inward, sitting upright or falling open, or to the side. Add a few larger leaves even farther down the branch in the same manner. Add small irregular pieces of outstretched 180 gram #568 dark brown crepe that have been lightly stained with red liquid concentrated watercolor where the leaves meet the branch for a more natural-looking transition.

Attach a leafy offshoot to the main branch by binding the bottom 7" of the offshoot and main branch together with an extra 7" length of stem wire along their intersection to round that area out. Bow the offshoot outward and upward, and finish the bottom in a similar manner to the rest of the branch. Trim the bottom of the branch, if needed.

leaves by flower type

BOUGAINVILLEA

MORNING GLORY

CARNATION

ROSE

DAFFODIL

POPPIES

PEONY

COSMOS

DANDELION

ZINNIA

ECHINACEA

DAHLIA

EUCALYPTUS

RANUNCULUS

MARIGOLD

MAGNOLIA

leaf details

Here are a few general tips to help you with the individual leaf details that follow.

- Etch a line into the paper along a ruler at the appropriate angle to use as a guide for cutting the straightest line possible for the inner leaf edges when needed.

- Use 24-gauge green cloth-covered stem wire set in tacky glue up the centerline of the backs of the leaves, positioned $\frac{1}{16}$" below tips and extending 4" past bottoms. Hide wires between overlapping edges of leaf blades, if desired. Be sure the wire is secure before attempting to fold, cup, or stretch the leaf. When attaching leaves to thicker flower stems, trim the 4" leaf stems down to ¾" long so they will be less visible at the flower stem.

- Match paper grain direction when laminating leaf paper. Cut the leaf blades out after the paper is laminated for better results.

- Olive green doublette and outstretched 100 and 180 gram moss green crepe paper are suitable for any leaf. Leaves can vary in size, shape, color, and texture depending on season and region, so adjust as you see fit.

BOUGAINVILLEA

Templates: 1A to 1E

Paper: Olive green doublette, darker side up.

Special Instructions: Crease leaves along center ribs, undulate edges by stretching. Curve leaves downward at tips or keep flat. Leaf stems should be ¼" to 1½" long, depending on leaf size.

Attachment: Attach to bougainvillea clusters with floral tape. For longer vines, attach leaf stems to each other with floral tape or strips of olive doublette in staggered, rotating, opposing pairs, interspersed with bougainvillea clusters.

CARNATION AND GREEN TRICK DIANTHUS***

Templates: 2A to 2D

Paper: Outstretched 160 gram olive or 100 gram moss green crepe.

Special Instructions: None.

Attachment: Attach leaves in opposing pairs below ¼"-tall rounded dark-green floral tape bumps protruding $\frac{1}{16}$" from the stem.

For carnations, attach a pair of 2A leaves ⅜" below the calyx, followed 3" down by an opposing 2B pair, rotated on the stem, continuing down similarly with larger leaves.

For Green Trick dianthus, attach 2A leaves at the base of the flower without a bump, then continue down in a similar manner as the carnation. Bend leaves to swoop up from the stem, curve in waves or bend under. Wrap the stems with dark-green floral tape or crepe.

DAFFODIL AND DOUBLE DAFFODIL

Template: 3

Paper: Olive green doublette, darker side facing out.

Special Instructions: Place the template at the top of two layers of doublette crepe and cut around, extending the edges down past the template the full height of the paper. Laminate together, embedding a 24-gauge stem wire down the middle. Trim the edges, fold lightly inward along the center wire, and twist gently lengthwise.

Attachment: Locate tips of leaves near the center of the flower head, wrapping the bottom ¼" of the leaves and stalk with paper to match the leaves. If a leaf connection lower on the stem is desired, cut taller leaves from outstretched 160 gram olive or forest green crepe.

PEONY

Templates: 4A to 4E

Paper: Olive green doublette laminated to outstretched 100 gram green tea crepe, or darker outstretched 160 gram forest green crepe. Laminating two layers, even of the same color, can give these longer leaves a nicer quality.

Special Instructions: Bleed the colors from two-colored individual laminated leaf blades together by washing the lighter backsides with water. Let dry, then glue together and cup at the center to curl the sides inward a bit before attaching the leaf wire at the back. Overlap and tacky glue the bases of one 4A and two 4B leaves together per the templates, wrapping down the leaf stems 1" in crepe to match the face of the leaf. Point the leaves upward or bend back dramatically.

Attachment: Attach three-pronged leaves 1" to 2" inches down the stem with crepe stem wrap, usually in a lighter green. Attach smaller and single leaves tighter to the stem, closer to the flower, placing some at the base of the flower head. Soften leaf transitions at the stem with a small amount of red stain, if desired.

MORNING GLORY

Templates: 5A to 5C

Paper: Outstretched 180 gram moss green crepe laminated to outstretched 180 gram green tea crepe.

Special Instructions: Brush the stem wire with a light red stain and let dry before attaching. Crease the tip of the leaf inward, then bend the bottom ¾" of the center of the leaf backward and cup the sides upward to create a recess at the stem.

Attachment: Attach leaves on the stem wire 7" to 12" down from the flowers, or wrap several leaf stems into vines with outstretched 180 gram moss green crepe. Use only one leaf shape per vine.

ROSE

Templates: 6A to 6E

Paper: Olive green doublette, darker side up, 180 gram #600/5 green-yellow ombré crepe, or any green crepe, left creped or outstretched.

Special Instructions: Crease leaves along center ribs. Flatten, cup the back on either side of the rib for a slightly convex face, or bend the leaf wire to give it a wave. Leave edges smooth or serrate with tiny scissors, making small curved cuts downward and then inward parallel to the grain. See page 188 for rose leaf coloring, composite leaf construction, stem wrapping, and more.

Attachment: Attach where desired with floral tape or crepe paper strips.

POPPIES

California Tree Poppy*
Templates: 7A to 7E

Paper: Outstretched 100 or 180 gram moss green crepe.

Special Instructions: None.

Attachment: Attach 7A leaves in opposing pairs 1" below the flower, followed by 7B leaves rotated 1¼" down the stem. Continue as desired, spacing larger leaf pairs farther apart down the stem. Swoop leaves up and then bend tips back or forward.

Wrap the stem with outstretched crepe to match leaves. Stem can also be left bare.

Opium Poppy (Danish Flag, Lilac Pom-Pom, and Black Swan)
Template: 7F

Paper: Outstretched 180 gram #562 dusty green crepe.

Special Instructions: Add the smaller jagged edges freehand after cutting out the leaves. Pull your thumbnail along the back edges of the leaf to curl back slightly. Trim leaf stem to ¾" long, and cut ⅜"-tall slits at either side of leaf rib wire.

Attachment: Bend leaf wire back at top of slits and attach to stem 8" down from flower with light-green floral tape. Wrap the bottom of the leaf around the stem and secure in front with a dab of tacky glue. Pinch the leaf onto itself along the rib at the bottom and top. Bend the tip back slightly.

Oriental Poppy*
Template: 7G

Paper: Outstretched 180 gram moss green crepe.

Special Instructions: Adjoin two pieces of crepe as shown on the template. Attach 20-gauge green cloth-covered stem wire with glue along the seam and pinch paper around to cover the wire. With paper-covered-wire-side up, use the template to cut the larger segments of the leaf, then freehand the jagged edges. Cup each segment lightly with the pad of your thumb and pivot each slightly upward.

Attachment: Attach low on the stem with a bit of light-green floral tape. Place smaller segments from the top of the template closer to the flower.

Iceland Poppy*
Template: 7H

Paper: 100 gram moss green crepe.

Special Instructions: Adjoin two pieces of crepe as shown on the template. Tacky glue 24-gauge green cloth-covered stem wire to both the front and back of the seam. Use the template to cut the curving segments of the leaf. Cup the ends of each segment, overlapping each segment over the one above it, adding a touch of tacky glue to each to keep in place. Rub the stem with yellow chalk and blend with a brush.

Attachment: Attach low on the stem with light-green floral tape.

CHOCOLATE AND GARDEN COSMOS

The two cosmos flowers included in the book have distinctly different leaves.

Chocolate Cosmos
Templates: 8A to 8F

Paper: Olive green doublette.

Special Instructions: Assemble and wrap multiple leaf stems following the rose leaf instructions on page 188. Crease centerlines and bend leaves back slightly.

Attachment: Attach low on the stem with paper to match stem wrap.

Garden Cosmos
Template: Guide 8G

Paper: Outstretched 180 gram #600/5 green-yellow ombré or #562 dusty green or moss green crepe to match stem color.

Special Instructions: Cut thin, tapered slivers from strips of crepe, rotating your scissors with each cut from the same location without regard to grain direction. Piece together the fernlike leaf on a central stem wire following guide 8G, attaching the pieces together with little dots of tacky glue. Cover the front of the stem with thin slivers of crepe when finished, then crease the leaf inward and pull the ends back lightly over a skewer to curl. Bend the end of each leaf back slightly. Not for the faint of heart.

Attachment: Attach in opposing horizontal pairs low on the stem with stem wrap. Smaller fronds made from just a few paper slivers can be placed in pairs closer to the flower.

DANDELION**
Templates: 9A to 9D

Paper: Olive green doublette, darker side up.

Special Instructions: Cut a 20-gauge green cloth-covered stem wire that has been brushed with a bit of diluted crimson liquid concentrated watercolor to extend 1½" below your leaf. When the stain dries, glue the leaf edges together, leaving the top 2" open on the larger leaves, 1" open on the smaller. Tacky glue the wire up the face of the leaf and onto the bottom open blade. Overlap the top blade onto the wire with tacky glue to create a taper where the wire disappears between the two layers. Scrape off excess glue and, when the stem is secure, cup the leaf gently from the back on each side of the rib to make the face slightly convex and wavy. Curl some leaf edges back over a hat pin, and dust with yellow chalk. Bend the leaf into a subtle S-curve. Use the extra bottom wire to stand dandelions in a display, or clip off.

Attachment: Leaf independent of stem.

ECHINACEA
Templates: 10A to 10B

Paper: Outstretched 180 gram #600/5 green-yellow ombré or 100 gram moss green crepe to match stem color.

Special Instructions: None.

Attachment: Attach the base of leaf 10A directly to stem, 3" down from the flower, covering the wire with the stem wrap. Attach the larger 10B leaf in the opposite direction, down 2½". Swoop leaves up close to the stem, then outward.

EUCALYPTUS**
Templates: 11A to 11D

Paper: Olive green doublette with outstretched 180 gram #562 dusty green crepe, or outstretched 100 gram moss crepe with 180 gram #564 blue green crepe, or both sides outstretched bark paper (see page 55).

Special Instructions: Attach two leaf sides (such as 11A and 11B) along their inner curves and set the stem wire in glue along that curved seam. One at a time, glue two similar leaf sides to the first, in a different color if desired, smoothing over the center wire so that it resembles a rib. Lightly stain some edges and bits of the center rib with diluted crimson liquid concentrated watercolor or coffee.

Attachment: Attach close to the stem under the stem wrap, interspersed between eucalyptus pods.

MARIGOLD

Templates: 12A to 12E

Paper: Outstretched 160 gram grass-green crepe, or darker, if desired.

Special Instructions: Follow template 12A to adjoin two angled pieces of crepe, attach stem wire at the back, and cut tiny leaflets using 12A as a guide, bending inward a bit after cutting. For a larger leaf, cut, glue, and add wire to the individual 12B to 12E leaflets, using the templates as a guide to cut the serrated edges, then wrap the leaflets into a full leaf structure. Crease leaflets inward along their ribs and bend each back and up slightly, then bend the entire leaf back and up slightly.

Attachment: Attach the fernlike smaller 12A leaves closer to the flower, the larger leaves farther down the stem, covering the leaf wires with the darker stem wrap.

ZINNIA

Templates: 13A to 13D

Paper: Outstretched 100 or 180 gram moss green crepe, laminated to outstretched 180 gram #562 dusty green crepe.

Special Instructions: Cut out the laminated leaf blades and glue together. While still malleable, cup the bottom half of the leaves and crease each upper side inward by folding along the lines on the templates. Cut out the bottom slots and attach the leaf stem wires to the backs of the leaves. When the wire is secure, flood the face of each leaf lightly with water, then dab crimson liquid concentrated watercolor around the slot. Let dry before attaching to the stem.

Attachment: Bend the leaf wires back and slip the leaves around the stem in opposing pairs, the smallest leaves 1" down from the flower head, followed by a larger pair rotated down 4", continuing on in that manner. Secure the leaf wires with the stem wrap.

DAHLIA*

Templates: 14A to 14G

Paper: Olive green doublette, outstretched 160 gram forest green or 180 gram moss green crepe.

Special Instructions: Glue leaf wires at fronts of the green leaves and rub with yellow chalk. Cup the leaves inward and carve folded-looking vein lines into the faces with your thumbnail. For dark foliage made with forest green crepe, place 2 drops of crimson liquid concentrated watercolor onto a brush covered in Mod Podge, then quickly mix and spread the Mod Podge all over the front face of the leaf. It will dry almost purple-black and will have a nice sheen. Attach the stem wire to the backs of the darker leaves.

Attachment: Space smaller leaves 1" to 2" from the calyx and larger ones 5" and farther down the stem with green crepe or dark-brown floral tape to match the stem.

RANUNCULUS

Templates: 15A to 15C

Paper: Outstretched 180 gram moss green crepe laminated to outstretched 100 gram moss green crepe.

Special Instructions: Crease the smaller 15A leaves up their center ribs and bend back a bit at the tips, or leave flat. For larger composite leaves, flank one 15B leaf by two 15C leaves, overlap, and glue the bases together. Stretch the unwired portions with your fingers to smooth and bend back a bit.

Attachment: Attach smaller leaf bases directly to the flower stem staggered 1" to 2" from the flower. The larger composite leaves can be attached in a massive cluster or collar around the stem, 3" to 4" down from the flower. Attach leaf wires at the flower stem with the stem wrap, some leaves poking out perpendicularly, others swooping upward.

MAGNOLIA

Templates: 16A to 16C

Paper: Olive green doublette, darker side up, laminated to outstretched 180 gram #567 light brown crepe.

Special Instructions: After laminated leaf is assembled, coat the green face with Mod Podge. Let dry 5 minutes, then fold lightly to crease the bottom two-thirds of the center rib. Cup the back of the leaf at each side so that most of the front of the leaf is slightly convex, then cup the top 1½" of the face of the leaf at each side of the rib to be concave. Curl the edges all around the leaf back lightly on a hat pin or skewer, then flatten back out to lessen the effect. Wrap leaf stem wire with outstretched light-brown crepe, extending paper 1" below the leaf on the bottom 4" of wire. Form a pointed tip at the top. Glue the wrapped wire up the back of the leaf and recup the leaf as needed. Rub yellow chalk into the bottom center and edges of the leaf, blending well. For offshoot branches, trim the leaf sizes down ⅛" or so from those on the main branch to make them appear slightly younger.

Attachment: See magnolia branches on page 191.

* Suggests leaves that are more easily cut using crepe paper that has already been glued together, as opposed to cutting out the two leaf sides first and then attaching together.

** Suggests leaves that are more easily cut by tracing the templates with a felt-tipped pen 1/16" outside of the outline and cutting out the leaves inside the lines.

*** Indicates both of the above.

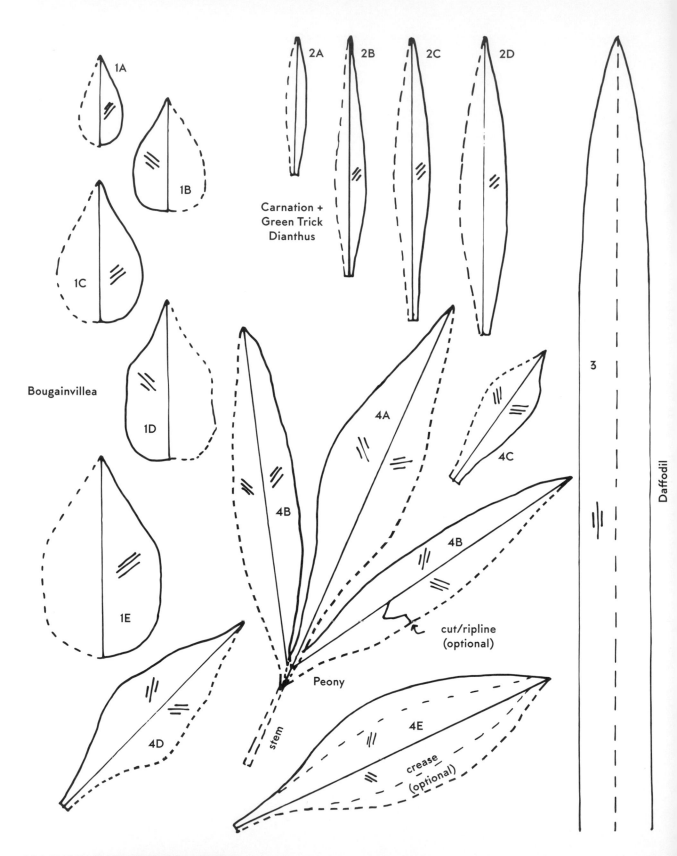

1A

1B

1C

Bougainvillea

1D

1E

2A   2B   2C   2D

Carnation +
Green Trick
Dianthus

4A

4B

4B

4C

cut/ripline
(optional)

Peony

stem

4D

4E

crease
(optional)

3

Daffodil

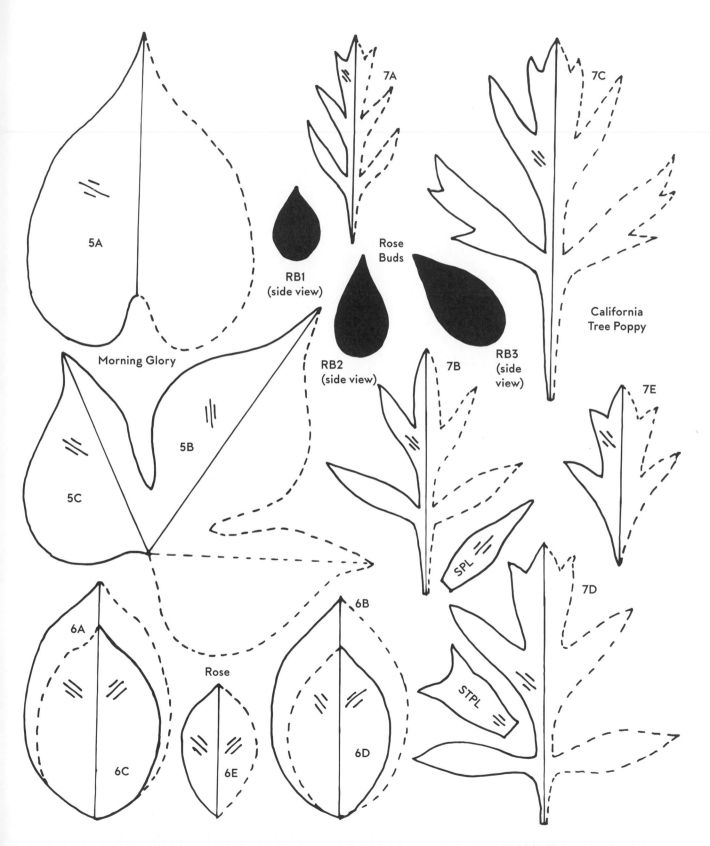

5A

Morning Glory

5B

5C

6A

6B

6C

6E

6D

Rose

RB1
(side view)

Rose
Buds

RB2
(side view)

RB3
(side
view)

7A

7B

SPL

STPL

7C

California
Tree Poppy

7E

7D

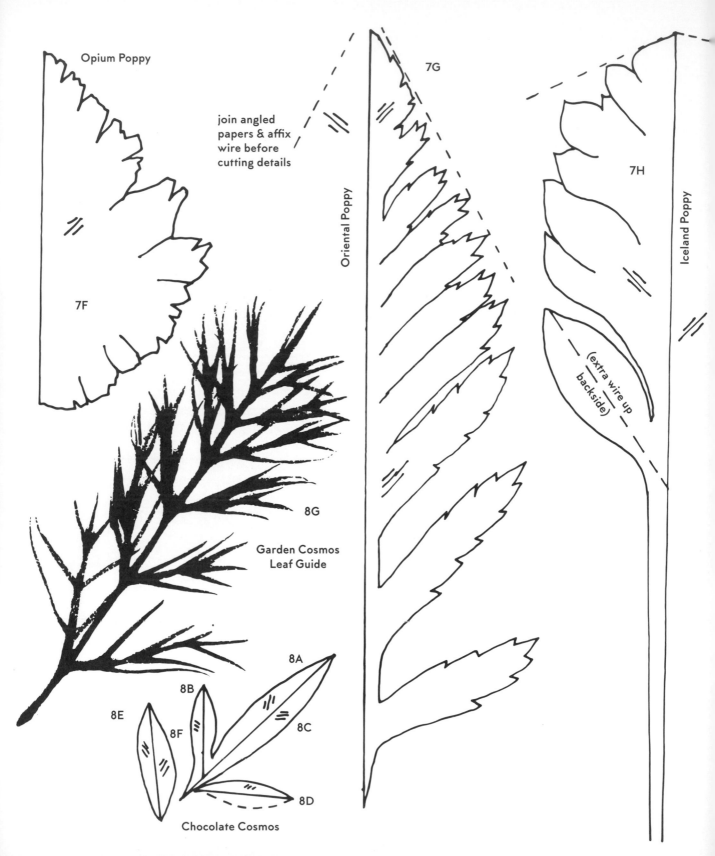

Opium Poppy

join angled
papers & affix
wire before
cutting details

7F

7G

Oriental Poppy

7H

Iceland Poppy

(extra wire up
backside)

Garden Cosmos
Leaf Guide

8G

8A

8B

8E

8F

8C

8D

Chocolate Cosmos

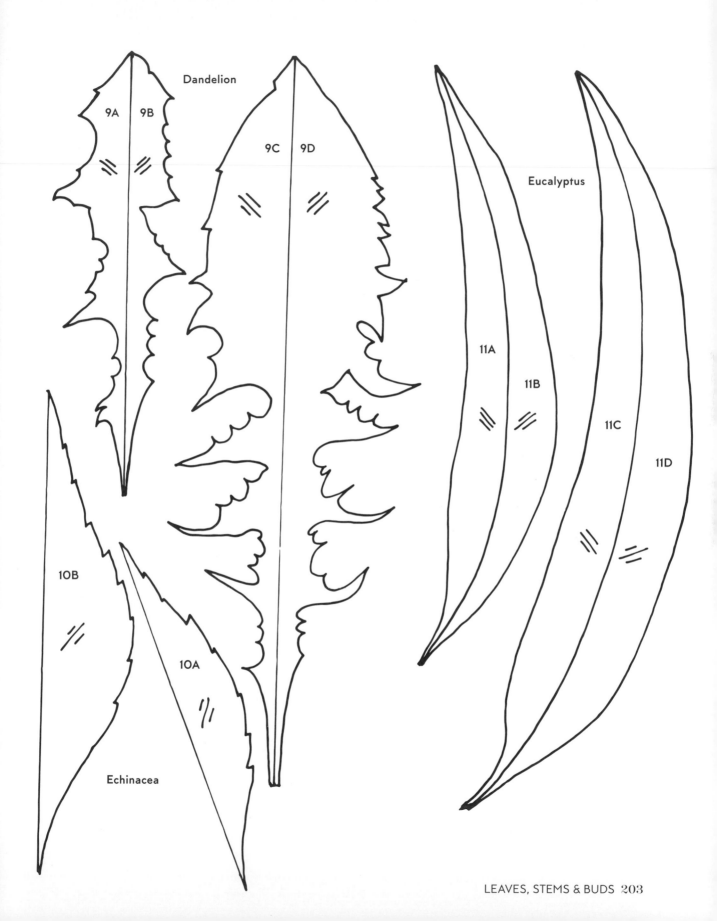

Dandelion

9A 9B

9C 9D

Eucalyptus

11A 11B

11C

11D

10B

10A

Echinacea

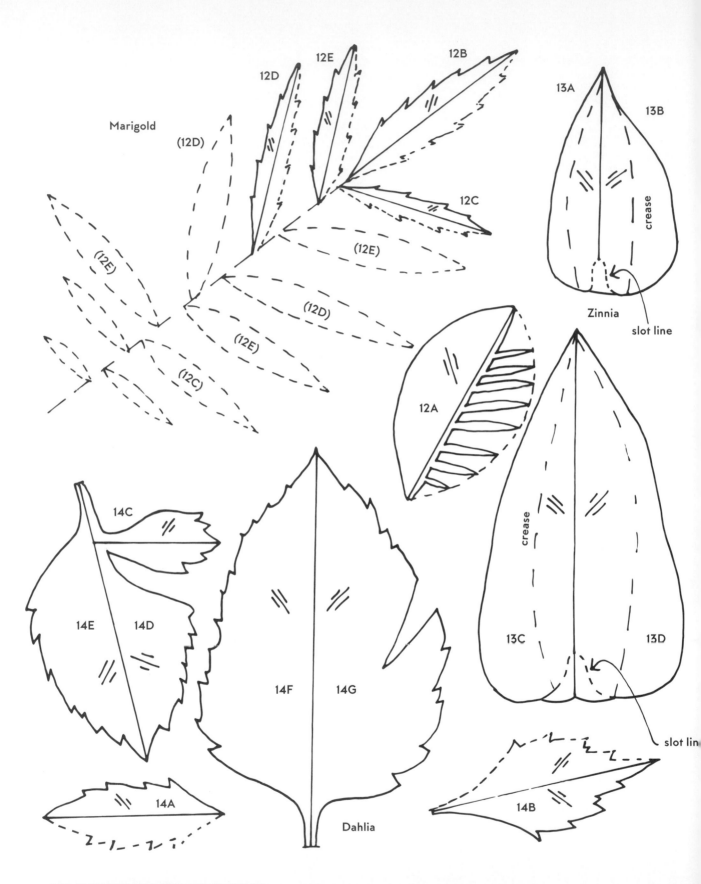

Marigold

12D

12E

12B

(12D)

(12E)

(12E)

(12D)

(12E)

(12C)

12C

12A

13A

13B

crease

Zinnia

slot line

14C

14E

14D

14A

14F

14G

Dahlia

crease

13C

13D

slot line

14B

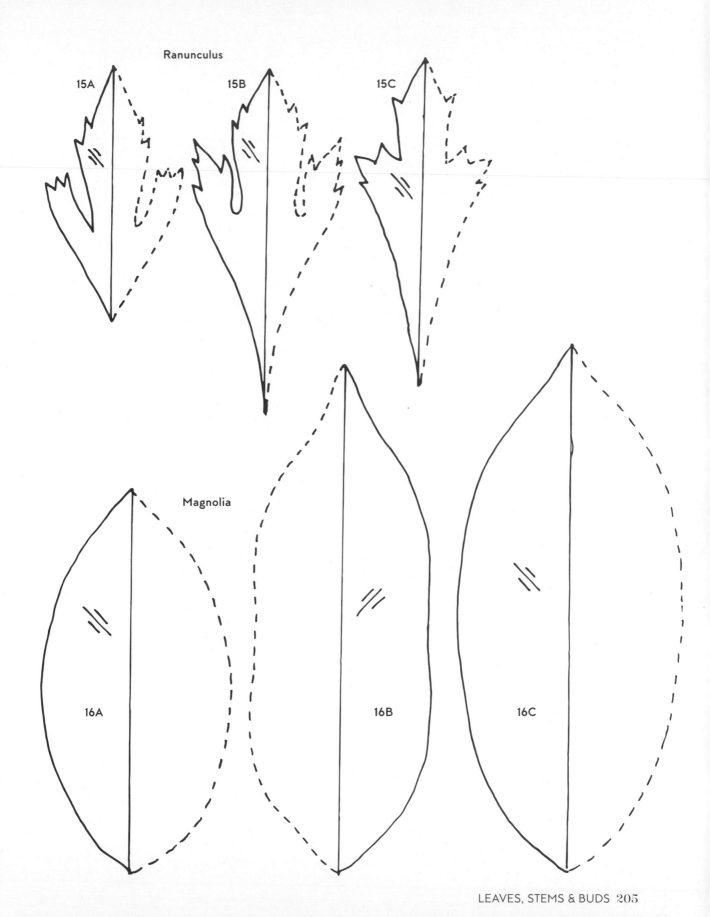

Ranunculus

15A   15B   15C

Magnolia

16A   16B   16C

CHAPTER 4

things to wear & things for your hair

on wearing paper flowers

To me, there is no better use for a paper flower than to wear it. If well made, paper flowers can go from the wedding ceremony to the dance floor, and on to last as invaluable mementos of very special days. I wear my favorite paper flower headpieces time and time again with little wear and tear. Wearing paper flowers can be as simple as tucking them behind your ear, but it is also great fun and so beautiful to pile them up high on your head. I made my first paper flowers for a headpiece for a performance, so this is where it all started for me.

There are more species and color options than I could ever dream of when it comes to paper flowers, realistic or imagined. In these wearable projects, I've used flowers from this book to give suggestions of flower combinations and how to construct them to wear. Use these as a basis to design and create your own floral masterpieces. As with all things paper flowers, keep your creations away from flames and moisture.

daisy chains
& flower garlands

A flower chain could not be simpler. Cut the stems of the flowers you want to use to the lengths you desire, and loop the end of each stem around the base of the next flower head, twisting around itself to close. If you are planning to make flowers for use around your head, use 18-gauge brown paper-wrapped wire (which is sturdy and malleable) for the stems, bending them to contour to your head. Leave your flowers oriented on the stem as-is, with a slight bend to face frontward if you are seeing much more stem than flower. Flowers in the Asteraceae family, like dandelions, cosmos, and zinnias are best suited for this type of chain and crown.

I spent four months in northern India a lifetime ago studying architecture. In my time there, I became very enamored with the marigold and carnation garlands I saw at many of the temples and wedding processions I was lucky enough to encounter. Flower garlands have religious, tribal, and cultural significance all over the world, like the Hawaiian lei and the Thai malai, and in Portugal during the Festas de Povo, where the streets are literally covered with strand after strand of paper flowers. No matter where you come from, with its repetition and abundance and color and texture, a flower garland can be a beautiful and festive thing.

CONTINUED

The marigold tutorial on page 131 gives instructions on how to build the flower around a wooden skewer in such a way that when the skewer is removed it leaves an undetectable hole through the face of the flower all the way to the back, making it easy to string. You can adapt that technique for flowers such as carnations, dahlias, roses, and double bomb peonies, among others. Some will take a bit of trial and error on your part. If you are finding it hard to remove the skewer, try wrapping the end of the skewer very tightly with a 1"-tall strip of paper without adhering it to the skewer before attaching the petals. Even if some petal bases become attached to the skewer below the strip, it should come out with just a bit of twisting.

Using a piece of thin, bent stem wire as a needle, you can thread yarn, jute, ribbon, or other string of your choice through the holes to create your garland. Beads or other items can be placed between the flower heads for decorative purposes, or to space the flowers farther apart, tie a knot below each flower's calyx in the desired location along the garland.

boutonnières

For our small backyard wedding, I made the boutonnières from fresh clusters of lily-of-the-valley, my mother's favorite flower, and they were all but completely shriveled by the time we got to dinner. So I can appreciate a paper flower boutonnière not only for its heirloom status, but for its continuous fresh face while being worn.

Any smallish paper flower will do, but pay attention to where and how the boutonnière will be attached. If the flower has a large calyx, like that of a carnation or marigold, you can obscure the calyx by sliding it down through the buttonhole of the lapel. If there are no buttonholes and you are required to pin the boutonnière to the front of a lapel, you might want to avoid tall, prominent calyces and stick with flowers like bougainvillea, hybrid tea roses, pom-pom poppies, or zinnias. Or, maybe try the playful version of a baby Green Trick dianthus shown on the following page. I made several of these for the groomsmen in a wedding a few years ago and I just love them. You can follow steps 4 and 5 to turn any paper flower into a sweetly finished boutonnière.

CONTINUED

BABY GREEN TRICK DIANTHUS BOUTONNIÈRES

Tacky glue

Hot glue

100 gram green tea crepe paper

16-gauge green cloth-covered stem wire

Any color floral tape

¼"-wide satin ribbon

Corsage pins

1 Cut ten 1"-tall by 8"-long TYPE I continuous strips of 100 gram green tea crepe paper. The guide for TYPE I strips can be found on page 147.

2 Create a small hook in the top of the stem wire. Apply a thin layer of tacky glue along the uncut bottom of one strip and wrap around, concealing the top of the hook and keeping the bottom of the strip level. Repeat with a second strip, setting ⅟₁₆" down from the first, then repeat again with another four strips, their bottoms all aligned with the second strip. Let sit for 10 minutes to set up, then brush the pointed fringe out and downward to begin to form the rounded shape.

3 Wrap the remaining four strips around at the intersection of the vertical base and the fringy parts of the strips, filling in so that by the last strip the base will be concealed and the bottom strips will lay horizontally. Let set up 5 minutes, then groom into a messy, somewhat globular shape, which should be somewhere around 2" wide and 1½" to 2" tall.

4 Cut the stem to be 3" long and fold it back up with a tight fold at its halfway point, creating a 1½"-long folded stem. This length is nicely proportional to this size flower, but see what looks best to you if using other specimens. Cut an additional piece of stem wire ¼" shorter than the folded stem, and secure it to the other two pieces of wire with hot glue, located at what will be the front face of the stem. This makes the finished stem look more rounded and helps the bottom look more tapered.

5 Use tacky glue to secure the end of your ribbon to the back of the stem ½" up from the bottom with the length of ribbon dangling down. Bring the ribbon down to cover the bottom of the stem, then begin to wrap tightly upward in a spiral, exposing almost the full face of the ribbon as you go. Overlap each layer just enough to conceal the stem wire, ⅟₁₆" or so, leaving no gaps. Wrap around the base of the flower twice and tie off tightly, pulling the end of the ribbon downward. Trim the end of the ribbon off at a nice angle. Provide two corsage pins crossed through the double layer of ribbon at the top of the stem. Bend the head of any flower forward between 5 and 10 degrees to ensure it sits properly on the lapel when pinned.

bouquets

If you don't know by now, paper flowers do not behave at all the way real flowers do, no matter how real they may look. They don't conform. They crash into each other instead of moving out of each other's way and are stiff, not supple. I wrestle with the flowers constantly, especially when making bouquets.

One morning I was telling all of this to my florist friend Monica, who has a great flower shop just a few blocks from our flat. She always has the best flowers and gets me specimens from the flower mart whenever I need them. She gave me some great advice. As she grabbed a magnolia branch from a vase with one hand, she said to find a structure, or framework, which would serve as the foundation to build the bouquets around. She began placing the flowers in the spaces created between the leaves and the intersections of the branch. And she was right, it worked beautifully. If you'd prefer to use something smaller than a magnolia branch for your bouquet, the structure on a multiflowered stem of roses can be helpful, as can the spaces in between a cluster of bougainvillea.

The flowers included in the bouquet shown on the following pages are: magnolia branch with forked offshoot (page 191), Cafe au Lait dinnerplate dahlias (page 153), Echinacea Supreme Milkshake coneflowers (page 123), chocolate cosmos (page 93), Bride's Dream Japanese form peonies (page 41), antique and cream colored carnations (page 29), a pink-and-peach Benary's giant zinnia (page 141), and a "brighter" faded Coral Charm peony (page 169).

Finish your bouquet by binding it together with a wide ribbon of your choice, tied with a simple, fresh knot.

crowns

The most joyful workshops I teach are the ones where we turn the fruits of our hard work, our handmade paper flowers, into beautiful flower crowns. While symbolic across the centuries and around the world for all types of occasions, we don't need to follow a lot of rules when it comes to purely decorative flower crowns. They are as interesting, flattering, and beautiful covered in perfect, pink roses as they are with the most random assortment of colors and flowers, and every last flower in this book works beautifully in a crown.

That said, when building a flower crown, it is helpful to think not only about your choice of flowers, but also the composition. There can be a hierarchy, anchoring the crown with larger flowers flanked by smaller ones, or you can keep a similar profile throughout. Placing flowers off to the side feels much different from setting them dead center on your forehead. I place my flowers from temple to temple, ear to ear, or in a cluster on one side, but you can ring your entire head with flowers if you'd like.

The brown paper-wrapped wire base on page 229 is suitable for most crowns. Paper flowers are easier to attach to the crown if they are built on thinner, more bendable stem wires, so do so if you can. Attach the flowers with their faces visible, twisting the stems around the base tightly several times before cutting away excess wire. With the crown on your head, frequently check for bare spots and exposed stem connections between the flowers using a handheld mirror above your head reflected in a larger one, or ask a friend to help. Readjust the flowers and fill the bare spots with more paper flowers or greenery when needed. The crown will become tighter as flowers are added, so loosen with the adjustable clasp at the back. When all of the flowers are attached, secure them to the base with a little hot glue. For a more finished-looking crown, cover the twisted flower stems by wrapping between the flowers with a piece of beautiful ribbon secured with a bit of hot glue, letting loose ends flow down at the back of your head for a romantic look.

CONTINUED

Here are a few of my favorite ways to adorn a crown.

BRIDAL CROWN

This is a great chance to make any flower in this book in white, whether it grows that way or not. Picture white dandelions or morning glories along with your roses and ranunculus. A monotone crown in any color makes such a statement, and in all white it is unmistakably bridal.

COSMOS CROWN

For an ethereal look, bend a tall, staggered bouquet of chocolate or garden cosmos around one side of the temple to the back of the head and attach the flowers to the crown base where they naturally fall.

CREEPY CROWN

Create a variety of flowers, like dahlias, roses, and carnations, from black crepe paper. Mount flowers from ear to ear, and finish with a veil of black millinery birdcage netting attached behind the flowers, draping down over your face.

LEAF WREATH

Cover the crown base with any and all of the leaves in this book, twisting them to lay flat or angle them outward in a more three-dimensional manner. Overlap the leaves a bit all around the crown so there is no visible beginning or end.

BOUGAINVILLEA BRIDGE

Use bougainvillea to bridge between larger flowers in a patch across your forehead for amazing texture or to fill in between other flowers in a crown with individual clusters. Make the inner buds smaller and less noticeable, letting the bracts get all the attention.

fascinators

Here are two jaunty wearables, the large, single-flowered fascinator and the teardrop-shaped fascinator, both meant to be worn at the side of your head just above your ear, with the tip facing upward on the teardrop-shaped fascinator.

SINGLE-FLOWERED FASCINATOR

This fascinator is different from the other headpieces in this book in that the flower is built directly onto the base, not attached after it is made. The best candidate for this fascinator is the Dinnerplate Dahlia on page 153, altered slightly to attach to the circular fascinator base on page 229.

Cover the base in outstretched crepe to match the petals, then wrap a 1¼"-tall by 12"-long strip of fine, spindled fringe onto itself and hot glue to the top center of the base to act as the flower's center. Follow the remaining steps of the dahlia tutorial to form the flower, bending the petal bases farther back to accommodate being glued to a horizontal surface instead of a stem, tucking bent-back outer petals deep under the petals before them as you work from center to edge. Secure the outermost petals to the base at a downward angle, adding filler petals as needed, completely obscuring the base.

Japanese form peonies (page 41) and faded Coral Charm peonies (page 169) can be adapted in a similar manner. The Japanese form peonies may need an extra row or two of petals to make them look full while covering the base at the same time.

CONTINUED

TEARDROP-SHAPED FASCINATOR

Use a crepe paper–covered base as described on page 231 for the following two teardrop-shaped fascinators. Remember to attach the felt lining and headband to the underside of the base after the flowers are affixed.

Flat Layout

Select flowers that sit flat or are relatively small, like bougainvillea, small poppies, cosmos, dandelions, and zinnias. Decide where they will be placed on the teardrop base, then, with your scissors, poke holes the size of the stem or flower base underneath each. Thread the flowers through the holes, interlocking and overlapping to fit, making sure some of the flowers overhang the base to soften the edges. Adhere each flower to the backside of the base with hot glue, tying stem wires together when helpful and trimming away the excess. As with flower crowns, paper flowers are easier to attach to the fascinator base if they have thinner wires, but it is not essential.

Eucalyptus Cascade

Flowers built on thin wires that look nice while pointed down, like eucalyptus in dirty white or hot pink, can be dangled from the teardrop fascinator base in a dramatic cascade. Create what amounts to a large, staggered cascade of tassels using 10 to 20 eucalyptus tufts (page 127) made with long 6" to 8" stem wires. Arrange the tufts into a cascade configuration on your work surface, starting with just a few that will be held at the top of the teardrop shape, and more bountiful as it descends in order to conceal the bulk of the base. Wrap the cluster tightly with stem wire just behind the top tufts to secure, and fold all of the stem ends down where they are wrapped together. Decide on which side of your head and face the cluster looks best and slip the folded stems over the top of the teardrop to one side or the other of the tip, adjusting the eucalyptus tufts to sit properly. Bend the stems in sharply, trim off excess lengths and hot glue to the bottom of the base securely, avoiding the centerline of the base where the headband will run.

headdresses

The idea for these wonderful floral headpieces came from a consultation with a beautiful soon-to-be bride named Courtney a few years ago, who asked me for a "headdress." This conjured up all sorts of images, but what *headdress* actually meant in the end was that a crown just wouldn't do. She wanted height, spikiness, and an interesting form. In short, she wanted to wear a pile of flowers on her head without ever worrying about them falling off on her wedding day.

The headdress I ended up making was absolutely stunning on the bride, a combination of something regal and something whimsical. It was made from five dinnerplate dahlias, six carnations, and four dozen bougainvillea clusters, all in white. The bride added a veil in the back, and the bridesmaids wore matching bougainvillea clusters in their hair. A year later I displayed the piece during my residency in the de Young Museum in San Francisco on a long-necked mannequin head, where the public loved it as much as we did.

What follows is a description for how to construct a design of this nature on the headdress base from page 231, but it is clear to see that you can adapt this headdress for any pile of sturdy flowers in any color for any reason. The sky's the limit.

When preparing flowers for your headdress, use the sturdiest blooms at the base, avoiding single-layered flowers that have no girth. Marigolds, dinnerplate dahlias, carnations, and all of the pom-pom flowers in this book are good choices. Most of these flowers need to be built on thicker wires, so, when possible, add a thinner doubled-up 24-gauge cloth-covered stem wire interlocked very securely in the center of the flowers next to the thicker stems. When the flowers are finished, clip away the thicker stem wires and use the thinner wires to wrap flowers onto the headdress base. Keeping the backs of flowers as flat as possible will help with easier attachment as well.

CONTINUED

Lay out your flowers before assembling your headdress to see how they interlock and to study the physical and color composition all at once. I prefer to have two flowers at the front center as opposed to one, which can look like a headlamp. Set your bottom flowers to cover the front edge of the base completely, then thread the stem wires through the sinamay fabric and over to a wire edge of the teardrop and wrap tightly. Cut away small slivers of sinamay along the front and back sides of the bases for easier stem wrapping, and use hot glue to keep the flowers in place and stable.

Continue to attach flowers to the base and pile atop one another with a combination of hot glue and wires. Try it on often while you work to check fit and design. Bring the flowers to the end of the teardrop bases, or continue down the wire over the ears for a romantic look.

The higher up you go, the more you have to cover at the backside. Bougainvillea is a fantastic cover, especially when made with unstretched crepe paper for strength and with wires running up the backs of the bracts in hot glue, allowing them to be bent and adjusted for better coverage between other flowers.

When finishing the piece, check to be sure the inner workings are hidden from the outside. Tacky glue the bottom petals of the front flowers down to conceal the edges of the base. I prefer to leave the underside of the base and the inner tangle of wires unlined, for simplicity as much as for overall lightness. Store your headdress hanging upside down or on a mannequin head to preserve the shape of the petals.

bases for headwear

These four bases can be used to build a wide array of jaw-dropping headwear. Each can be adjusted for both child and adult head sizes. Sources for millinery bases, hat elastics, and elastic headbands can be found on page 16.

CROWN BASE

Hot glue

Two 18" lengths 18-gauge brown paper-wrapped stem wire

Fold one end of each length of stem wire back 2". Interlock and twist each end of the wire around itself three times to create two interlocked loops. Hold the interlocked area one-third of the way down your forehead, placing it where you know it will be hidden by flowers. Wrap the wires back around your head and fold them over each other so the crown feels snug but not too tight. Remove the wire from your head and create an adjustable clasp at the back by twisting one end into a secure loop while leaving the other as a simple hook, trimming away excess wire. Tuck the loose hook end under to hide it.

CIRCULAR FASCINATOR BASE

Hot glue

3½"-diameter circle of corrugated cardboard

Crepe paper to match flower

Felt

Hat elastic

For a fascinator base you can build a single flower onto directly, cut a slit from the edge to the center of the cardboard circle, overlap the edges of the cut ¼", and hot glue into place. Using hot glue, cover the convex top of the base with outstretched crepe paper to match your flower, wrapping it down around the underside ¾". Cover the underside of the base with a circle of felt in the color of your choice, holding the edge of the felt in ¼" from the rim. Make two small holes in the base directly opposite each other, in about ¼" from the rim. Insert the metal brad located at each end of a hat elastic into the holes from the underside, letting them sit flat atop the circular base. Obscure the brads with your fascinator flower.

CONTINUED

CROWN

CIRCULAR FASCINATOR

TEARDROP-SHAPED FASCINATOR

HEADDRESS

TEARDROP-SHAPED FASCINATOR BASE

Hot glue

Teardrop-shaped
4"-wide by 7"-long
sinamay fascinator base

Crepe paper to
match flower(s)

Felt

Fabric-wrapped
elastic headband

If you are planning on adding something lightweight to your teardrop-shaped fascinator, you can modify the instructions for the circular fascinator base to cover the top and bottom and attach a hat elastic. I usually use this base for heavier clusters of flowers, so I like to give it a sturdier elastic headband to keep it in place on my head. Using hot glue, cover the convex top of the base with outstretched crepe paper to match your flower, wrapping it down around the underside ¾". Be cautious, as the hot glue will seep through the underside of the sinamay material as you work. You will attach the felt lining and headband to the underside after the flowers are attached, as you want to obscure the stem wires of the flowers used on the fascinator with the felt. Cut a teardrop shape from felt in the color of your choice, ¼" smaller than the teardrop-shaped base. Secure the elastic headband in place by pressing one spot on the headband into a dime-size pool of hot glue in the middle of the concave side of the base using the middle of the felt shape. This is the only place the headband should be attached to the base; the rest should be allowed to stretch freely. The headband should be aligned down the center of the teardrop base, from pointy tip to center of wider, rounded end. Apply hot glue to either side of the headband to attach the rest of the felt, creating a glue-free channel where the headband sits. Pull each side of the headband to make sure it can stretch freely after the glue cools.

HEADDRESS BASE

Hot glue

Two teardrop-shaped
4"-wide by 7"-long
sinamay fascinator bases
(other longer shapes and
sizes can be used as well)

Upholstery needle
and embroidery thread
in color to match
teardrop bases

16-gauge green cloth-
covered stem wire

This easy base provides the framework to build a headdress of many larger flowers that will make a huge splash. Sew the centers of the two rounded, wired edges of the teardrop bases together securely with an embroidery or upholstery needle and thread. Poke the end of the stem wire through the pointed end of one teardrop, bend it back down 1¼", and twist onto itself with pliers. Sit the two teardrop-shaped bases just above your hairline, bend the wire down around the base of your head and back up to the pointed end of the other teardrop. Poke through the teardrop base and cut away most of the excess wire, leaving 2" to bend down as the adjustable hook.

CHAPTER 5

giant paper flowers

about giant paper flowers

My giant paper flowers, or "heads," as I like to call them, started off with humble beginnings, as piñatas, which is why their bases are made from papier-mâché. I wanted to make giant, pink, fluffy floral piñatas to hang upside down, fill with candy, and smash apart, but after I made my very first one I knew they were far too pretty to whack with a stick.

What makes these paper flowers so special is the result of a little reverse engineering and an epiphany. It's the secret to everything and it's on the next page: the inverted base. Instead of building the flower on top of a balloon-shaped papier-mâché piñata form, it occurred to me to lop off the top, flip it over, set it back in upside down, and use that concave bowl as a way to let the petals grow from the inside of the flower out, just like a real flower's would. The inverted base also allows you to create flowers that have deeply recessed or cavernous centers and is suitable for constructing almost any multi-petaled flower. Simple to construct, but making all the difference, the inverted base is probably the best idea I've ever had in my life.

I use metallic latex balloons under the papier-mâché, as they have the thickest walls and are the most durable. Mixing a little tea tree oil in with the flour and water freshens the smell, but it is optional and needs to be mixed in well, as direct contact can break down the latex and cause the balloon to pop. I suggest making several bases during one papier-mâché session, as inevitably a few balloons will pop or spring an air leak while you are working. Allow three or four days of lead time when constructing the papier-mâché bases to ensure each layer dries completely before applying the next.

This chapter contains instructions on how to make the base, the tutorial for a giant paper peony, which clocks in at around 26" in diameter, and the templates. There are also a few suggestions on how to adapt the tutorial to create other giant specimens. Use these gorgeous flowers as decor for weddings, parties, and other celebrations, or simply as beautiful art for your home. You can even tie one under your chin and wear it as a costume or a giant derby hat, if you'd like.

I could talk at length about my deeper thoughts about giant paper flowers, but I'll just give a little testimony here. Flowers smell good to pull us closer and look pretty so that we want to propagate them. They are dynamic on the stem and in the vase, changing with the season or by the day, here one month and then gone for the next eleven. So when a flower is enlarged, everything around it grows. They make people feel wonder, delight, surprise, and amusement. Inspiration. And almost always an exchange of energy occurs. It doesn't matter if the flower is hanging on a wedding photo backdrop with a hundred other flowers or hanging on a museum wall. These giant flowers draw stories out of people. I've seen it over and over in my fine art career. Presented with a larger-than-life specimen, nine times out of ten a person will be compelled to talk about what their relationship to the natural world is or share their personal memories, or just chat about flowers. It's truly a beautiful thing. You will see.

papier-mâché base

- Newspaper
- Large metal or glass bowl
- 3 to 5 cups flour
- Water
- Tea tree oil (optional)
- 12" silver or gold metallic latex party balloon
- Colander or small bowl
- String
- Pushpin
- Embroidery thread
- Measuring tape
- Marker
- Scissors or X-Acto knife
- Upholstery needle
- Hot glue
- 180 gram #600 white crepe paper (optional)
- Small or large picture or monkey hook (optional)
- Phillips head screwdriver (optional)
- Picture wire (optional)

1 Rip sections of a newspaper into 1½"- to 2"-wide strips. In a metal or glass bowl, mix 1 cup of the flour with 1 cup plus 2 to 4 tablespoons cool water with your hands until it feels like very thin pancake batter, then thoroughly mix in 5 to 6 drops tea tree oil, if using. Blow up a metallic latex balloon as large as you can without thinning the walls significantly and set in a colander or on the rim of a small bowl to hold it as you apply the newspaper strips.

One at a time, submerge a newspaper strip in the flour mixture. Hold at one end over the bowl and wipe downward between two fingers to leave just a small film of flour and water on both sides. Carefully place the strip on the balloon and smooth down. Repeat all around the balloon, running strips in every direction, overlapping randomly. Smooth the surface down as you go, and thin the flour mixture with more water when needed. Cover the balloon completely, then hang from a string around the tied-off end for 24 hours to dry, keeping away from heat sources and stoves. When dry, cover with a fresh layer of papier-mâché, and then a third and final layer 24 hours after that. Wait until the last layer is completely dry before proceeding to step 2.

2 To cut the rounded end off evenly, insert a pushpin into the center of the rounded end of the balloon and tie a 12" piece of embroidery thread below the head of the pin. Use a measuring tape and marker to mark on the thread approximately 5" down from the pin and, then, laying the thread against the balloon, mark the papier-mâché 5" down from the pin every ½", all the way around. Connect the dots with your marker. If you need to, relocate the pin until you get a perfectly level line around the balloon. Cut along the line with scissors or an X-Acto knife, remove the deflated balloon, and invert the cut rounded end back into the form like a bowl. Sew into place around the perimeter with embroidery thread and an upholstery needle, then cover all of the stitches and the rim with hot glue.

3 Make marks 6" down from the sewn upper rim all around the form. Connect the dots and cut along the line to remove the pointed end. Cut the extra papier-mâché from the pointed end into 1½"- to 2"-tall scraps and strips and hot glue them around the bottom rim of the base for reinforcement. If a finished look is desired, line the interior with outstretched 180 gram #600 white crepe paper.

4 To hang the base flush with the wall, wedge the back rim of the base into a large picture hook. To prepare the flower for suspending from above or for extra-secure wall mounting, use a Phillips head screwdriver to punch three holes 1⅛" up from the back rim 9" apart, then add a second hole 2¼" to the right of each of the first holes. String picture wire on the outside of the base between the closer-together holes, then inside the base between the holes that are farther apart, tying off the wire tautly. Hook the inner wires on a monkey hook or small picture hook or stretch the wire to fit inside a larger picture hook with the rim for extra security.

1

2

giant paper peony

Hot glue
(100 to 200 mini sticks)

1 roll 180 gram #548
light pink crepe paper

8 or 9 rolls 180 gram #569
pale pink crepe paper

Papier-mâché base
(page 236)

1 Cut nine GPP1 petals from 180 gram #569 pale pink crepe paper and three from 180 gram #548 pale pink crepe paper. Save any excess paper from cutting petals for the smaller GPP6 and GPP7 petals in step 5. Carefully stretch the top portion of the petal on either side of the split so it is flat and not ruffled along the top edge, moving down the petal on each side of the split to stretch the paper evenly. If the top edges become too wide or square, trim them a little bit to round them again. Cup the center of each petal just below the split very lightly, then fold and crease backward along the petal's center line, so the two top edges flutter a little bit like wings. Run a light line of hot glue quickly down the back of the petal in the crease from the bottom of the split in the petal to the base, then scrunch the bottom 1½" around the glue to gather it. Repeat with the remaining eleven petals.

Test the height of three petals in the base before gluing, adjusting their heights by bending the bottom of their bases back so that their tops sit about 11½" from the bottom of the papier-mâché base. If you'd like a more recessed center, bend the petals to sit lower and slowly move them back up to 11½" by the end of step 2. Glue the three petals together at their center creases, leaving the bent bases free, then glue the bent bases down to the very center of the bowl, splayed outward.

2 Add the remaining nine GPP1 petals close to the first three at the center of the flower, hot gluing down at the bent bases and up the sides a bit to attach them together and keep them as vertical as possible. Position a few petals 1" higher than the others. Slide some between others if they fit naturally that way. Place petals in either shade of pink randomly whenever a step calls for two different pinks.

Cover the rim of the flower with 1½"-tall strips of outstretched pale pink crepe, then cut 15 GPP1 and 26 GPP2 petals, four of each from light pink crepe and the rest from pale pink. Stretch, cup, fold, and gather the GPP1 petals per step 1. Cup the GPP2 petals rather deeply, then gather the bottoms

CONTINUED

by overlapping one side of the base over the other and securing both front and back folds down with 2½" of hot glue. From the 26 GPP2 petals, glue together 13 loosely nested sets. The outer petal of each set should be smooth with a very slight stretch to the top edges on either side of the V. The inner petals should be an assortment of crumpled, smoothed, and top-edge-stretched petals.

Hot glue the petals as vertically as possible to the inner bowl of the flower. Step the winged single GPP1 petals up and down a bit. The cupped pairs of GPP2 petals should be bent at their bases and attached in the papier-mâché bowl to the bottom and up the sides as needed to cup over the GPP1 petals ½" to 1". The petals should be placed in a bit of a scramble, and several nested sets should sit one right behind the other or slightly staggered. Pivot some to the side and face others toward the center. The petals do not need to form a perfect circular perimeter. Inject or pour extra hot glue around any petal bases that are floating off the bowl due to how they were positioned.

3 Cut four final GPP1 petals and 14 final GPP2 petals, all from pale pink crepe. Bend the top edges of the GPP2 petals back very slightly over your finger. Groom and nest both petal types per step 2, but instead of bending the bases backward, glue them carefully to the inside face of the bowl so that the petals sit upright. Fill gaps and spaces where you can see the inside of the bowl with the GPP1 petals, and cup the nested GPP2 petals over the inner petals just a little bit.

4 Cut eight GPP3, 20 GPP4, and four GPP5 petals, all from pale pink crepe. Stretch, fold, and gather two of the GPP3 petals similarly to the smaller GPP1 petals, then stretch the tops of the other six GPP3 petals from the backside to curl back a bit and cup their bellies at their front

faces. Crumple two of these by gathering and squashing the convex side of the cupped portion, then smoothing back out a bit. Cup the GPP4 petals and cut ¾"-deep by ¼"-wide Vs in the tops of 12 of them, then crush the backsides of five of those. Two or three of the GPP4 petals without V cuts should be gathered at the top in a little pleat with hot glue to make it extra round and cupped. The four mitten-shaped GPP5 petals should be cupped at their centers and up the larger side of each, with the smaller side of each cupped lightly from behind at the top edge to give it some stretch and bend it backward.

The top edge of all GPP3 and GPP4 petals should be bent back a bit over your finger. Gather the bottoms of all step 4 petals by overlapping one side of the base over the other and securing both front and back folds down with 2½" of hot glue. Hot glue sets of nested petals with the more cupped GPP4 petals behind crushed or less cupped GPP3 and GPP4 petals. Attach the nested sets around the outside of the base, doubling up, staggering with each other, or turned slightly inward and slid between other petals. Hot glue open, cupped GPP3 and GPP5 petals behind some of the nested pairs, flaring out at their top edges, and slide the two folded GPP3 petals to fill in where needed.

The petals from this step should reach slightly above the inner petals, cupping over where possible and reaching to 13" maximum above the bottom of the papier-mâché base. These are the center petals that will project out farthest from the side walls of the base. Keep the petal bases straight when possible, but bend back, if needed, to fit around the flower. Attach them to the outer wall of the base densely enough that there are only small gaps between the petal bases around the perimeter. At the end of the step, the diameter of the flower should be about 15".

CONTINUED

3

4

5

6

5 I enjoy this step a lot. It really takes the peony from a rose or carnation look into peony territory. These little petals make the flower so special and fluffy, and if you cut, gather, and groom them all before attaching to the flower, it's not as much work as it sounds. Cut 50 GPP6 and 50 GPP7 petals from pale pink crepe. You will most likely need another 20 or so of each, but it is better to start with fewer. First, cut from scraps left over from steps 1 to 4 and then cut the rest from a roll of crepe, cutting through two to four layers of paper at once to save time. Cup the largest part of the GPP6 petals, then lightly stretch the top edge of the center section from behind to widen slightly and bend back a bit, then cup the rounded, outermost section, or "pinky," from the backside. Follow the same instructions for the GPP7 petals, but lightly stretch the back of the angled top edge of the "pinky" to slightly widen and bend back a bit.

Gather the bottom one-fourth to one-third of each of these petals with hot glue, then shape the petals into different types of tufts, some with the "pinky" secured to the backside, some pleated so they splay out more, some folded back onto themselves, some wide open, and some with the "pinky" bent toward the front. Gather them with hot glue along their bases in clusters of anywhere from three to eight petals, staggering so the bottom petals in a cluster protrude up to ¾" beyond the petals glued on top of them. Use these clusters to fill in the gaps between the larger petals around the perimeter of the bowl. Some clusters should extend out horizontally around 6" from the base, and others should angle upward with their tips up to 2" below the larger petals. These petal clusters do not have to make a consistent ring around the flower. Leaving spaces is fine, as long as the flower doesn't appear too unbalanced. If you need a place to affix petals that need to extend out or up, put a cluster of four or so tucked in closer to the base and use that as a base on which to stack other, longer-appearing petals. Keep adding until the flower looks balanced and the gaps between petals are filled, more or less.

Line the outside of the base with strips of unstretched light pink crepe.

6 Cut 30 more GPP3 petals from pale pink crepe. Cup both sides of the V as well as the belly of each petal. Stretch the top edges of 10 of the 30 petals flat and bend back slightly with your finger. Stretch and fold another 10 of the 30 flat, then crease and hot glue backward like the petals in step 1. Gather the bottoms of all 30 petals by overlapping one side of the base on the other and securing both front and back folds down with 2½" of hot glue. Set the petals between and below the smaller petals from step 5, bending the bases back and attaching each to protrude from the base between 6½" and 7½". Use the petals to fill in open areas, angling some of the folded ones up with their folded edges facing inward to help soften the transition between the upper petals and the smaller clustered petals. The lowest of these petals should protrude horizontally, only falling down slightly from gravity at their ends.

CONTINUED

7 Cut 50 GPP8 petals from pale pink crepe to start; you may need about 20 more. Cup each petal at its belly and on either side of the V cut. Stretch one or both top edges of 10 of the petals so they lay a little flatter or bend backward a bit, but a majority of the petals should cup upward, with a few draping downward on both sides to fill in gaps.

Fold the bottom 1" of each petal down into a tab. Pleat the center ¼" of that tab over itself and secure with hot glue. This helps stiffen the petal and reinforce the cupped bellies a little. Apply these petals with hot glue covering the tabs all around the flower, separating them from each other vertically by about ¾" to 1" and staggering randomly. The petals should always cover the cut bottom edge of the tabs above them, so be mindful of this, but do not line them up in a row one after the other. The petals should protrude from the flower horizontally. If you crowd their bases too close underneath each other, they hang down and don't sit correctly, and you will have to add twice as many petals to finish the flower. The bottom petals should sit about 1" to 2" from the bottom rim of the base and be layered and staggered enough to obscure the base when viewed sitting on a flat surface.

8 This peony can be modified in so many ways. You can take cues from the longer, spoonlike guard petals from the three peonies found in chapter 2 and add them at the bottom. You can eliminate some of the petals from steps 1 and 2, instead filling the bowl with large, spindled stamen fringe. You can use fewer flat petals and more cupped, or you could replace the smaller GPP6 and GPP7 petals with more GPP3 and GPP4 petals for a different profile. With a little practice, studying flowers in nature can give you big clues on how to adapt this tutorial for flowers like marigolds and chrysanthemums, carnations and roses.

7

8

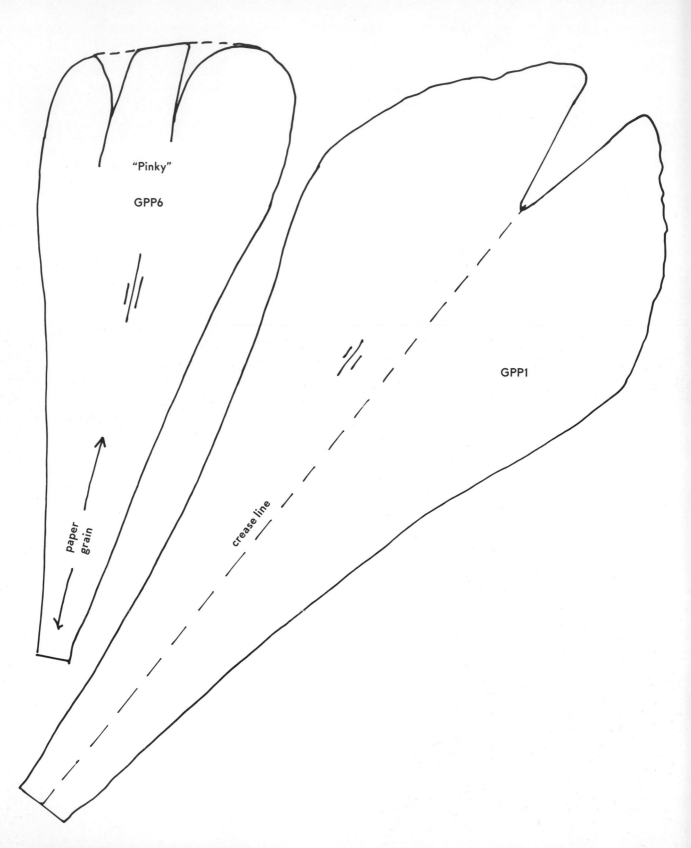

"Pinky"

GPP6

GPP1

paper grain

crease line

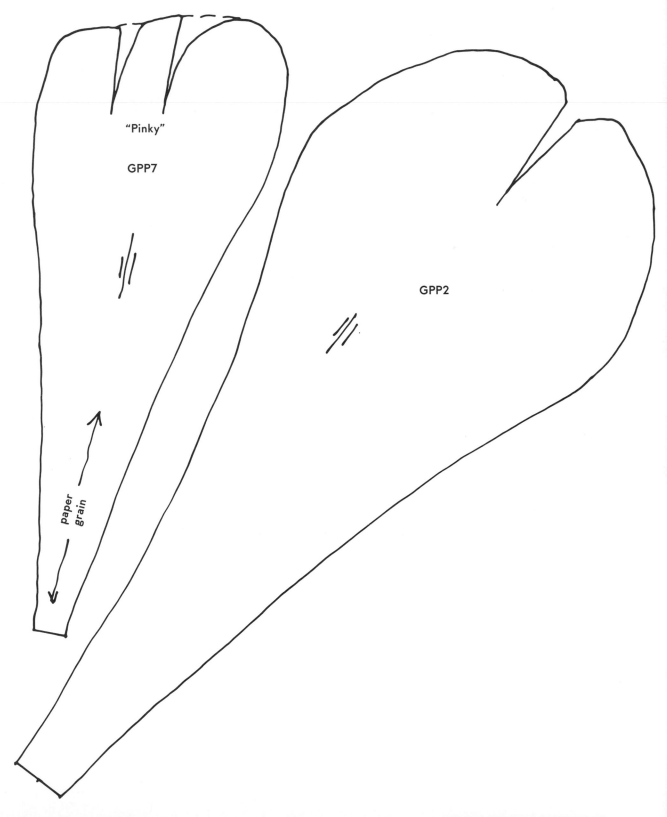

"Pinky"

GPP7

GPP2

paper grain

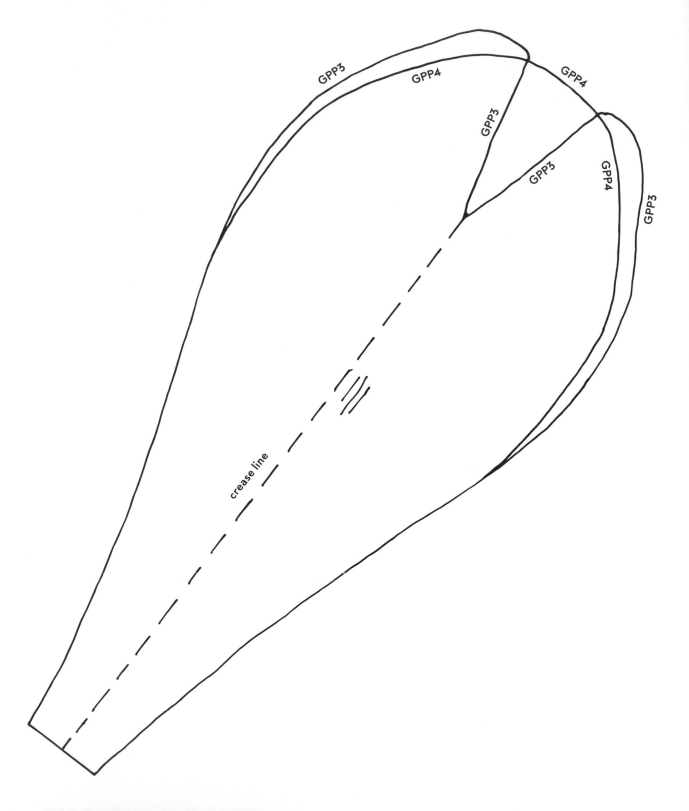

GPP3

GPP4

GPP3

GPP4

GPP3

GPP3

GPP4

GPP3

crease line

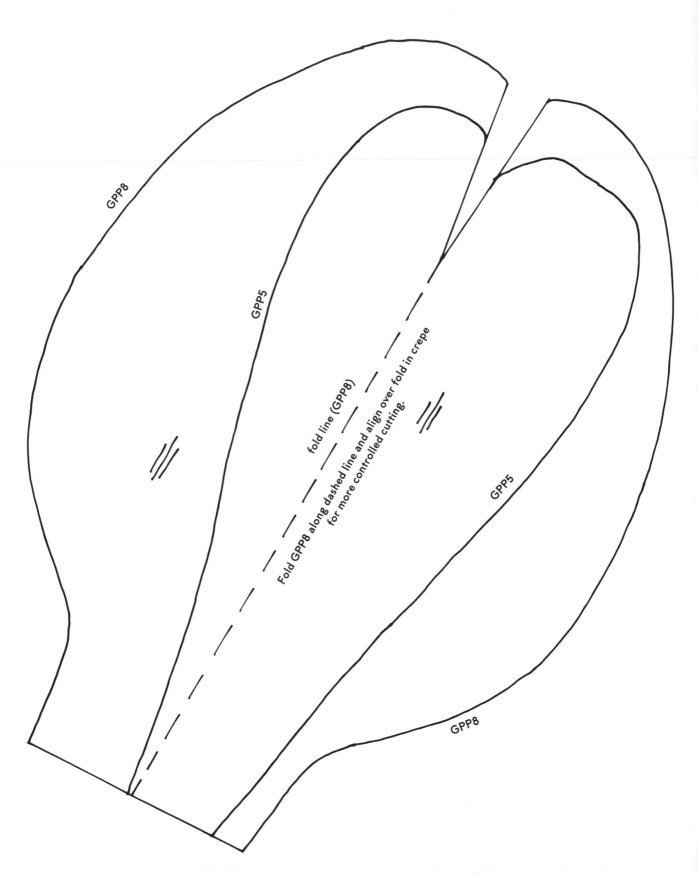

GPP8

GPP5

fold line (GPP8)

Fold GPP8 along dashed line and align over fold in crepe
for more controlled cutting.

GPP5

GPP8

acknowledgments

Writing this book was a staggering amount of work, so difficult that at times I wondered if I was doing it right. It was an experience my family and I will never forget. There are a lot of people who helped along the way and I need to thank, each one from the bottom of my heart.

Windy Dorresteyn, thank you for your expertise and your ear. There wouldn't be a book to begin with without you. We love you.

To my team at Ten Speed Press. I don't believe I could've been in better hands. Thank you to my editor, Kaitlin Ketchum, for your way with words and your way with me; to my art director and designer, Ashley Lima, for hearing and seeing my vision and sharing yours; and to editorial director Julie Bennett, for taking a chance on me.

Thank you to photographer, Aya Brackett, and her assistant, Alvina Wang, for the stunning photographs and finding such beautiful locations to take them. You helped to tell the stories I wanted to tell. Thank you to Natasha Kolenko, for your A+ styling skills and impromptu modeling, and to the people at Scribe Winery in Sonoma and the Starline Social Club in Oakland for letting us use every inch of your special facilities.

Thank you to Mason Hunt, who made essential, beautiful bits to help me fill these pages. To Aida Hassani for modeling with Stella, to Eleanor Gerber-Siff for "THE URN," and to Michael Merritt for making the beautiful vase on page 62.

Monica Lomas, friend and florist. Thank you for all the specimens, advice, and for listening to my exhausted ramblings about flowers.

To my brides, Courtney Cochran and Lilis Wu. Thank you for pushing me, and for lending me your treasured wedding items for these pages.

In no particular order, I need to thank these friends for all of the support they have given me in so many ways. Randy Wiederhold, Catherine Martin, Anna Branning, Robin Jakery, Kindley Walsh Lawlor, Marie Murphy, Paul Bibo, Stacy Shartzer, Kim Blake Prause and Mike Prause, Shannon Fairchild and Tom Randell. Thank you!

To Grace Bonney, Kevin B. Chen, Giselle Gyalzen, Jan Halverson and Danielle Krysa, the curators of and writers on my work, who have taken chances and helped to bring more attention to the fine art of paper flowers. Thank you all.

Marie Muscardini and Handcraft Studio School, thank you for holding up the craft community and being a friend. Brittany Watson Jepsen and The House That Lars Built, I have always kept my eye on my own paper, except when it comes to you. Thank you for all the beauty you give the world.

Mike and Chrissy Benson and Carte Fini Fine Italian Paper, the amount of support you have given me in exchange for so little amazes me. I will always be indebted to your generosity.

Thank you to my mother, Alexis Brown, a creative person and artist in her own right, who taught me endurance and commitment. I love you.

Thank you to my closest advisor and husband, David Vazquez, who gave so much so that I could become the artist I wanted to be. Thank you for everything, David. I love you.

And finally, to my beautiful daughter, muse, critic, and idea person, Stella Vazquez, and to my wonderful son, photographer, snuggle supporter, and paper scrap cleaner, Oliver Vazquez. Thank you for playing at my feet and skipping a summer while I wrote this book. You are part of everything I do, and I hope you feel it. I love you both much, much more than paper flowers.

about the author

TIFFANIE TURNER is a fine artist specializing in botanical-based sculpture, a Zellerbach Family Foundation grant awardee, and the creator of the large-scale crepe paper flower "head." She is also a licensed California architect, an amateur art exhibit curator, and an instructor in the art of paper flower making across the United States.

Her work has been exhibited at Tower Hill Botanical Garden, Bedford Gallery, Jack Fischer Gallery, the San Jose Institute of Contemporary Art, and at the de Young Museum in San Francisco during a month-long artist residency.

Tiffanie's work has appeared in *Vogue*; *American Craft*; the *San Francisco Chronicle*; and *O, The Oprah Magazine* and been featured online on Design*Sponge, The Jealous Curator, and Poppytalk, among others.

Raised in the woods of New Hampshire, Tiffanie now resides with her husband and two children in San Francisco, California, where she has lived for the past twenty years.

index

All rights reserved.
Published in the United States by Watson-Guptill Publications,
an imprint of the Crown Publishing Group, a division of
Penguin Random House LLC, New York.
www.crownpublishing.com
www.watsonguptill.com

WATSON-GUPTILL and the WG and Horse designs are registered trademarks
of Penguin Random House LLC

Library of Congress Cataloging-in-Publication Data
Names: Turner, Tiffanie, author.
Title: The fine art of paper flowers : a guide to making beautiful and
  lifelike botanicals / Tiffanie Turner.
Description: First edition. | Berkeley, California : Ten Speed Press, [2017]
Identifiers: LCCN 2017013232 |
Subjects: LCSH: Paper flowers. | Flower arrangement.
Classification: LCC TT892.T77 2017 | DDC 745.92—dc23
LC record available at https://lccn.loc.gov/2017013232

Hardcover ISBN: 978-0-399-57837-3
eBook ISBN: 978-0-399-57838-0

Printed in China

Design by Ashley Lima
Photograph on page 186 is by Ashley Lima.

10 9 8 7 6 5 4 3 2

First Edition